67- 11104 (11·14·68)

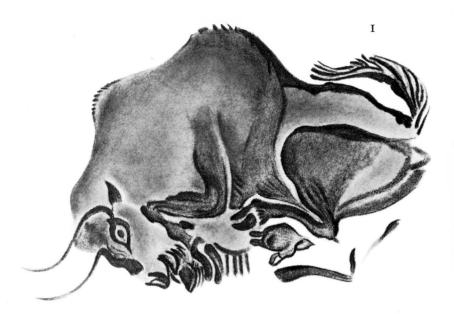

*Painted bulls. Altamira, Spain.*

*Cave paintings. Lascaux, France.*

*The Sorcerer,*
*carved and painted on*
*the wall of the cave*
*of Trois Frères, France.*

*The Venus
of Lespugue.
Musée de l'Homme,
Paris.*

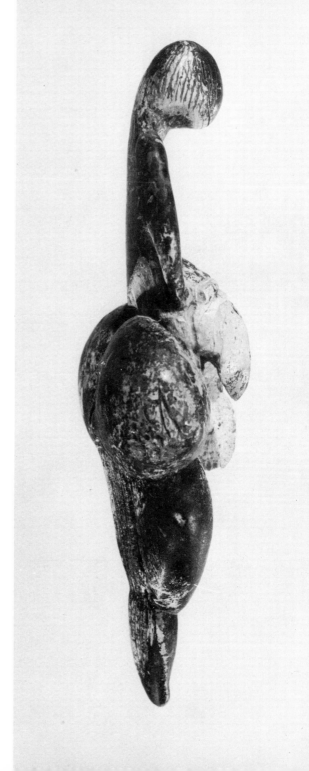

*Bison sculptured in clay.*
*Cave of Tuc D'Audoubert, France.*

*Azilian painted pebbles.*

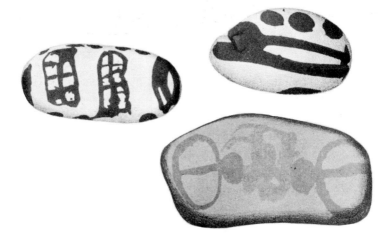

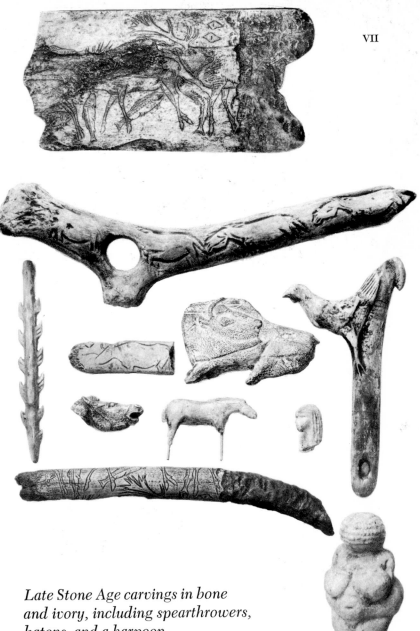

## VII

*Late Stone Age carvings in bone
and ivory, including spearthrowers,
batons, and a harpoon.
The statuette at lower right is
the Venus of Willendorf.*

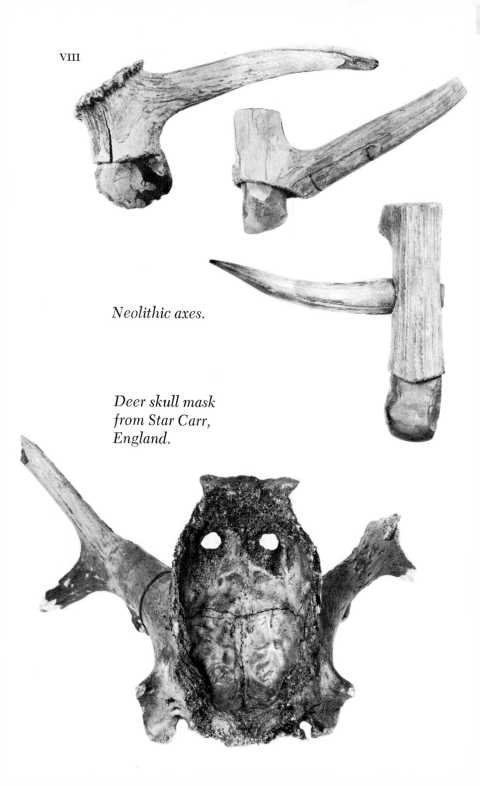

VIII

*Neolithic axes.*

*Deer skull mask from Star Carr, England.*

# The Morning of Mankind

PREHISTORIC MAN IN EUROPE

# THE
# MORNING
# OF
# MANKIND

ROBERT SILVERBERG

*Prehistoric Man in Europe*

NEW YORK GRAPHIC SOCIETY PUBLISHERS, LTD.

*Library of Congress Catalog No.*
*67–11104*
*Text Copyright © 1967 by*
*Robert Silverberg*
*Manufactured in the U.S.A.*
*Design by*
*Wladislaw Finne.*

Who can put limits on the past? Is it not infinite, as is the future? Where, then, is the man who has seen the beginning of any one thing? Where is he who will see it end? Let us not bargain over the duration of ages; let us believe that the days of the creation, those days that began before our sun, were the days of God, the interminable days of the world.

*Jacques Boucher de Crèvecoeur de Perthes, 1860*

# CONTENTS

# INTRODUCTION

The subject of this book is prehistoric man: his way of life and how we came to know about it. That's a sweeping statement that immediately needs to be explained. Obviously, no one book could try to sum up in two or three hundred pages all that is known about prehistoric man. Such a book would become a series of frenzied paragraphs, packing in so much information that there would really be no information at all. So the subject of this book, in fact, is the life of prehistoric man in certain parts of the world during a certain period of time. The prehistory of Europe from about 25,000 B.C. to the founding of the Roman Empire is our center of attention.

A great deal of the story of mankind lies outside those limits. The physical evolution of man—his gradual change from a primitive beastlike form to his present appearance—is not our topic here. Nor will

2 we do more than take the briefest glances at what happened to man in Asia, Africa, or the Americas. We will not devote much space to the birth of historic civilization in Egypt and Mesopotamia, either. Those all are fascinating stories, but they are beyond the boundaries here.

Why set such rigid limits?

There are many reasons, and they are not just the need to keep the story from overflowing the confines of a short book. Perhaps the most important is that the story of prehistoric man in Europe is a tale well worth telling, and one much less familiar than the story of the ancient Near East. The Solutreans, the Beaker Folk, and the Megalith Builders hold fascinations no less great than do the Sumerians and the Babylonians. Most of us know something about what took place under the bright sun of Egypt, but not enough about the events in the caves and dark forests of Europe.

Then, too, European prehistory tells the story of our own ancestors. Of course this is not true for all Americans, by any means. On any city street we can see the descendants of African kings and Chinese warlords, of Phoenician navigators and central Asian charioteers. But the founders of our nation came from Europe, and a majority of our people today trace their parentage from that continent. When we look toward the mammoth-hunters and village-builders of ancient Europe, we are looking toward our own forefathers' deeds.

There is also a good reason for beginning the story so close to our own day. It is hard to define "mankind," but most authorities now admit that human beings have existed for at least a million years. If we could think of that vast span of time as a single year, the scope of this book would cover less than two weeks out of that year. All the rest is prologue.

Now, the events of the first "fifty weeks" of man's stay on Earth are significant ones; but the actors in that drama were not men like ourselves in appearance. They were different from us in basic physical ways. Their very bones were unlike our bones. If they could be brought forward in time to walk among us today, those early men would seem strange, alien creatures. We owe them reverence, for some of them are our most distant ancestors. But it seemed best to begin this book with the rise of our own species of human being.

The word "prehistoric" deserves some explanation, too. Strictly speaking, there is no real gap between prehistoric and historic times. The flow of human events has always been continuous. We make an artificial division between the time when men learned how to write and keep records, and all that went before. It is a convenient division, but we should always remember how artificial it is.

In the Near East, prehistoric times ended about 3000 B.C. We know the names of Egyptian Pharaohs and Sumerian kings of that era; we have inscriptions that tell us of battles and rituals and daily life. But China remained prehistoric for another fifteen centuries, Greece for five hundred years beyond that, western Europe for a thousand years more. In the Western Hemisphere, we date the end of prehistoric times from A.D. 1492. Parts of Africa and some Pacific islands are still living in prehistory by most standards. We must not think, then, of an epoch of prehistoric darkness suddenly ending all over the world when some switch was thrown in Egypt to dazzle men with light. The different cultures of the world have crossed the border from prehistory to history at different places, over a period of thousands of years. And that border is so fuzzy and indistinct as to be practically meaningless anyway.

4    The danger in talking about "prehistoric" man lies in thinking that he was in any way less human than "historic" man. He could not read or write, true. But he could develop art, poetry, and religion. He could fall in love. He could take delight in the beauty of a sunset. He could value fine craftsmanship. He could dream, and hope, and make plans. We must not let the label "prehistoric" conjure up images of grunting, bestial savages. Some prehistoric folk surely *were* savage and barbaric; others were highly cultured, civilized in all important respects except that of being able to record their own history. The darkness that we imagine for the prehistoric past is mostly a darkness of our own sympathies and imaginative abilities, not a darkness that actually existed.

There were men before history. They lived and worked, argued and examined, loved and worshipped. No doubt they regarded themselves as the lords of creation and felt pity for the brutish savages of the even more remote past. They did not think of themselves as prehistoric or primitive. They were the noblest representatives of humanity in their part of the world—and, for all they knew, in the whole universe.

For the sake of a handy label, we have thrust all these prehistoric men into the same box. We have set up an artificial category that encourages us to think of them as somehow less than human. We slap the misleading tag of "cave men" on them and pretend that we have understood what they were like.

But it is wrong to confuse the achievements of a culture with the personalities of the individual members of that culture. We have surrounded ourselves with complicated things—electricity, jet planes, television, telephones—that would seem like miracles to the man of twenty thousand years ago. (Or to the man of two hundred years ago!) But that does not mean that we are superior, either as a group or as individuals, to those earlier men. We know more tricks than they did; but they were not beasts, nor are we gods. What should astonish us, as we look at our ancestors of the prehistoric past, is not how different we are from them, but how very much the same.

ROBERT  SILVERBERG

# 1
# MAN
# DISCOVERS
# HIS
# PAST

In 1868 a dog exploring a Spanish hillside found a cranny big enough to slip through. The dog wriggled between the rocks until it reached a dark cavern within the hill. Thereupon it set up a loud barking, until its master, a hunter, came to its rescue. The man tugged at heavy boulders until he had opened a passage wide enough to allow the trapped dog to emerge.

There was nothing special, so far as we know, about the dog. But the cavern in the hill was extremely special, and when it finally was explored it served to touch off a major upheaval in the way men thought about their ancient forebears. The cave at the hill of Altamira shattered a proud and boastful idea: that mankind has marched steadily upward from dreadful savagery. For the contents of that cave demonstrated that humanity had reached a high

8    level of culture at a time when man was supposed to have been a miserably brutish creature.

What was found at Altamira amounted to a humbling and uncomfortable lesson. Such lessons, of course, are never absorbed gratefully. The world did not want to hear what Altamira had to say; and the world was cruel to the man who brought it the disturbing news of what the cave contained.

He was Don Marcelino de Sautuola, a handsome, aristocratic Spaniard who owned the land on which the hill of Altamira rose. As the wealthiest and most highly educated man of his district, Don Marcelino was looked upon virtually as a prince by the peasants who lived and worked on his vast estate. He spent his time administering the affairs of his property, and in his leisure devoted himself to studies. Geology was his chief interest. He kept in touch with the latest geological research, and made frequent field trips to other parts of Europe. Naturally, he was keenly interested in the geological background of his own lands, and carefully collected rock specimens and soil samples in his native province.

When Don Marcelino was forty-four years old, in 1875, he learned of one place on his estate that he had not yet explored: the cave at Altamira. Since its accidental discovery seven years earlier, no one had entered the cave. A workman told Don Marcelino the story of the dog that had slipped through the crack in the hillside, and Don Marcelino decided to investigate further. He paid a visit to the hill, a mile and a half from his home.

Laborers rolled away the slabs of stone that blocked the mouth of the cave. By torchlight Don Marcelino saw a narrow cavern stretching far into the hillside. While removing the rocks at the entrance, the workmen came upon sizable caches of yellowed animal bones, many of them split lengthwise. Don Marcelino showed these bones to his friend Don Juan Vilanova y Piera, the professor of geology at Madrid University. Vilanova recognized them as the remains of certain extinct animals once common in that part of Europe, such as the giant stag, the wild horse, and the bison. He suggested that men had split the bones open to get at the tasty marrow they contained. Since most authorities agreed that those animals had died out thousands of years before, Don Marcelino knew that his cave must have been inhabited in the distant past.

Some rummaging near the cave entrance failed to produce anything more significant than split bones, and Don Marcelino turned to other studies. In 1878, though, he visited Paris and attended the Second Universal Exhibition, a great world's fair. One of the most fascinating exhibits was a display of prehistoric objects found in the caves of France—stone tools made by ancient man, knives and axes and scrapers and arrowheads of flint. Some of these stone tools had been found associated with bones of the same kinds of animals found at Altamira. Don Marcelino's interest in the cave was rekindled. Thinking that he might be able to form his own collection of ancient weapons and tools by digging there, he began a full-scale excavation in the cave early in 1879.

Blocks of stone had fallen from the roof of the cave, filling the narrow passage and making it impossible to penetrate deeply. Progress was slow as these fallen slabs were hauled away. As he worked his way inward, however, Don Marcelino's digging yielded an archaeological treasure-trove. More bones were found, and objects much like those he had seen in Paris: stone knives, awls, arrowheads, and scrapers. There were also some curious shells encrusted with deposits of black or dark red pigment. Deep within

10 the cave he found the skeleton of a cave bear, a gigantic extinct animal that had lived in Europe at a time when the climate was very much colder than it is today. He also discovered a side cavern, the roof of which was just a few feet above the floor at its mouth, gradually rising until after some distance it was possible to stand upright. This cavern ended in a chamber about sixty feet by forty. Huddling under the low roof, working by the flickering light of his torch, Don Marcelino saw that the floor of this chamber was covered with the ashes of ancient fires and by bits of bone and shell—signs that man had lived there. He gathered some specimens and returned to the main cavern.

Several days later Don Marcelino's young daughter Maria asked if she could come to the cave with him. He let her accompany him. She grew bored, though, watching her father patiently scratching in the dirt for pieces of stone and fragments of bone. While he worked, little Maria wandered off toward the low-roofed cavern, carrying a lamp.

Moments later she hurried back, in wild excitement. *"Papa! Mira, Papa!"* she cried. *"Toros! Toros pintados!"* Come look, Papa! Bulls! Painted bulls!

"Where?" Don Marcelino asked.

She pointed upward. He quivered with astonishment as he saw the incredible murals on the roof of the cavern. Though he had spent hours in the cave, he had never once thought to look upward. He had always walked or crawled warily along, keeping his eyes on the ground so that he would not miss some scrap of bone. Now he beheld a wondrous sight. Everywhere on the cavern ceiling were vividly painted animals, in life size, glowing with color so warm it seemed they could have been painted just days before. Here was a herd of massive humped bison, grazing, running, sleeping, standing. Here

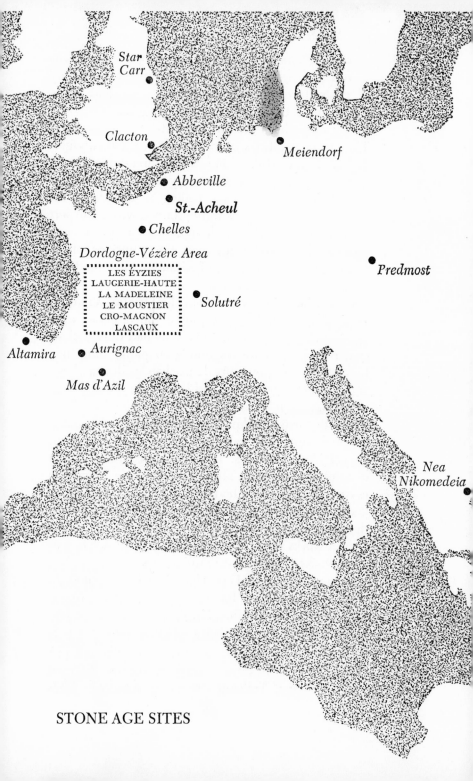

Star Carr

Clacton

Meiendorf

Abbeville

**St.-Acheul**

Chelles

Dordogne-Vézère Area

LES EYZIES
LAUGERIE-HAUTE
LA MADELEINE
LE MOUSTIER
CRO-MAGNON
LASCAUX

Solutré

Predmost

Altamira

Aurignac

Mas d'Azil

Nea Nikomedeia

STONE AGE SITES

12 were wild horses and charging boars, prancing beasts in red and brown and black, a stupendous gallery of portraits of the creatures that once had made Europe their home. (*Photograph, page i.*)

Nor were these the awkward attempts of savages. They were paintings by the hands of masters, vigorous and powerful. Some were three-dimensional, because the artists had cunningly made use of bumps and shallows in the cave ceiling as backdrops for their work. The animals were grouped with an expert sense of composition, although in some places one artist had worked right over the paintings of an earlier man. The animals of Altamira were rendered with stunning artistic skill.

Don Marcelino summoned his friend Vilanova from Madrid, and they explored the fabulous cave together. They saw how the artists had drawn charcoal sketches before beginning to paint; and they found the paint pigments themselves, yellow and red and brown minerals that had been ground to powder and mixed with bison's blood. They discovered places where the artists had pressed their own hands against the wall and outlined them with spattered paint, almost like signatures. It was a cave of wonder, a cave of amazement. The animals whose likenesses cavorted on the walls had died out, as far as anybody knew, five thousand or ten thousand or even twenty thousand years before. Here were mankind's oldest known works of art, then. But they were not beginners' works. They were masterpieces.

It happened that Don Marcelino had a guest in his house, a skillful but penniless French painter. Don Marcelino commissioned this man to make exact copies of the Altamira paintings, as illustrations for the book he was going to write about them. In 1880 the book was published: *An Account of Certain Prehistoric Discoveries in the Province of Santander.*

It described the paintings and the related flint and bone objects found in the cave, and set forth the claim that they were relics of prehistoric man.

It was a claim that the scientific world could not and would not accept. The ugly accusation of hoax was raised. Primitive man, the authorities said, had been a slow-witted creature hardly more civilized than a gorilla. Clad in furs, living in caves, ignorant of science or literature or the arts—how could such rude beings have painted the masterpieces of Altamira? These elegant, graceful bison and boars were clearly the work of expert modern painters who had studied at the academies of Paris or Madrid or Rome, and who knew how to produce exciting artistic effects. Why, as recently as the year 1400 the best painters of Europe had not understood how to impart such lifelike characteristics to their work. Only after Leonardo da Vinci and Raphael and Titian and the other masters of the Renaissance had attacked the problems of art could such works be possible. Here was this unknown Spaniard making so bold as to say that the barbarian huntsmen of long ago could equal the skill of Leonardo!

It was impossible to accept the authenticity of the Altamira murals. To do so would be to admit that in the morning of mankind there had been men with great artistic talents which had later been lost— progress in reverse. And those who believed in the steady upward climb of man from the caves were shaken and angered by the findings of Don Marcelino de Sautuola.

Emile Cartailhac, professor of prehistory at the University of Toulouse, denounced the paintings as frauds without bothering to make the trip from France to Spain to view them in person. A French engineer named Édouard Harlé actually did go to Altamira, examined the paintings, and also learned

*14*   that Don Marcelino had had a French painter as his houseguest at the time of the discovery. That seemed sufficient proof of the fraud to Harlé, and he went back to Paris to expose Don Marcelino's chicanery.

Later in 1880, Professor Vilanova attended the International Congress of Archaeologists in Portugal and defended the Altamira paintings against these attacks. He brought forth an array of arguments for their authenticity. No living artist, he said, could have had such detailed anatomical knowledge of the extinct animals. He showed the lumps of pigment and the shells that had been used as palettes, and insisted that they had been found in the same levels of the cave as the split bones of the long-dead animals. Finally, he declared that some of the paintings were coated with a thin layer of stalagmite, which could only have been deposited over many centuries.

It should have convinced the assembled scientists, and perhaps it changed the views of some of them. Most, though, continued to believe that the paintings were a hoax, or at least refused to accept them as genuine. Don Marcelino was crushed by the attacks on his honor. Bewildered, embittered, he died in 1888 at the age of fifty-seven. His defender Vilanova died five years later. The reputations of both men were stained by the charges against them.

In 1894 and 1895, the French archaeologist Emile Rivière, working in a cave called La Mouthe, found new animal paintings similar to those of Altamira. In some places, the paintings were partly buried by deposits of bones and stone tools—another proof of their great age. Clearly they were genuine, and therefore the ones at Altamira must also be the products of prehistoric man.

Other cave discoveries followed. By 1902, Don Marcelino's most stern adversary, Professor Cartailhac of Toulouse, had given in. In a paper called "The Grotto of Altamira: Confession of a Skeptic," he belatedly admitted his error. Don Marcelino's wonderful paintings were truly ancient after all. Cartailhac paid an apologetic visit to Don Marcelino's daughter Maria, the actual discoverer of the paintings, now a married woman. He asked her to forgive him for the wrongs he had done to Don Marcelino.

"These unexpected paintings . . . are in every respect magnificent," Cartailhac wrote. "However distant these primitive people may have been from us in time, we feel near to them and closely related in the same cult of art and beauty. We need not blush to call them our ancestors."

The lesson of the cave at Altamira was a hard one to swallow because it challenged some of man's fondest assumptions about the upward curve of progress. That was why it took more than twenty years for the scientific world to accept the paintings as genuine.

For the ordinary person, it was even more of an effort. When Don Marcelino de Sautuola published his report on the cave in 1880, he was striking the latest in a heavy series of blows against the popular view of man's past. All during the nineteenth century such blows had been landing with increasing force. The public had been asked to believe:

That the world was millions of years older than the Bible said it was.

That man had existed for many thousands of years in a state of brutal ignorance.

That the men of the ancient past had been physically different from modern man, much more ape-like in appearance.

Those ideas had been accepted reluctantly at best,

*16*　but by 1880 they were in wide circulation. Now came Don Marcelino to turn everything upside down with a new discovery: that somewhere in the supposedly brutish past, great artists had decorated the walls of the caves. Small wonder that people were confused and angry, at first. Later, of course, they came to understand how the cave paintings fitted into the picture of man's past that was beginning to emerge. But Don Marcelino was long dead by that time.

Sometimes an idea is so simple and obvious that no one wants to believe it. It takes a series of powerful jolts, like the blows of a wrecker's ball, to demolish a faulty structure of elaborate and incorrect theories and allow the truth to find its place.

The idea that mankind's past stretches back for many thousands, even millions, of years, is one of those concepts that had a difficult time finding acceptance. To us it may seem obvious. We know—because we have seen the evidence in the museums—that many sorts of primitive men walked the earth long ago, and fashioned clumsy tools from stone and bone, and gradually invented the skills and techniques that produced the great civilizations. And we do not find it hard to believe that it took a long time to develop those skills and techniques.

It was not always so obvious, though. Men had a truth to guide them—the literal statements of the Bible—and they preferred to cling to those statements, no matter what evidence to the contrary might come to the surface.

In the year 1650, an Irish archbishop named James Ussher announced that the creation of the world had taken place in 4004 B.C. He arrived at that precise figure by adding up the life spans of the important figures in the Bible, generation by generation, right back to Adam. The archbishop's computation of the

world's age was generally accepted throughout the
Christian world. Many editions of the Bible printed
today still give Ussher's dates in the margins of the
pages.

Almost everyone, it seems, was willing to believe
that the world was less than six thousand years old.
The known historical records went back to the great
days of Greece and Rome. Before that, scholars
knew, first Egypt and then Persia had ruled the
world. Noah had built his Ark in 2349 B.C. As for all
the skills of mankind, they had been perfected quite
soon after the time of Adam: the raising of crops,
the building of cities, the use of metals. These were
the generally accepted "facts."

For men who believed that God had guided mankind personally, often appearing and giving instruc-
tion, it was not difficult to think that progress had
been so swift. If God could create the heaven and
the earth in six days, it was reasonable to think that
six thousand years was enough time for man to build
a complex civilization.

Troublesome objects kept turning up, though, that
introduced certain doubts.

Men digging the foundations of new houses often
found the bones of strange, giant creatures in the
earth. No animal known had such bones. An explanation was produced: that these were the relics of
creatures that had lived before the great flood of
Noah's time.

A good many crude pieces of worked stone were
unearthed, too. They appeared to be axes, choppers,
and spear points. Were they relics of a period before
man knew the use of metals? The Bible said nothing
about a time when men had fashioned tools from
stone. It did speak of Tubal-cain, the great-great-
great-great-great-grandson of Adam, who was described as "an instructor of every artificer in brass

18    and iron." If man had known how to use metal so
soon after the Creation, the era of stone tools must
have been extremely brief. Yet these clumsy stone
axes came to light almost every time a spade was
thrust into the ground. How could there possibly
have been so many of them?

To account for the mysterious tools of stone, some
churchmen in the Middle Ages suggested that they
were weapons that had fallen to earth during the
"war in heaven" between God and Satan. The stone
objects were nicknamed "heaven axes." Later, they
came to be called *ceraunia,* or "thunderstones," when
the theory gained favor that the "heaven axes" were
formed by lightning striking the ground. The one
thing that no one cared to believe was that they were
the tools of human beings who had lived thousands
of years before.

A few bold voices were heard. Late in the sixteenth
century, an Italian physician named Michael Mercati
wrote, "Most men believe that *ceraunia* are produced
by lightning. Those who study history consider that
they have been broken off from very hard flints by a
violent blow, in the days before iron was employed
for the follies of war. For the earliest men had only
splinters of flint for knives."

A French scholar named Armand Jussieu declared
in 1723: "Looking at the shapes of these pieces . . .
which until now have always been taken for thunderstones and for something mysterious, we scarcely
could hesitate now to recognize [them] as tools."
Others in the enlightened eighteenth century agreed
with the opinions of Jussieu. Grudgingly, the guard-
ians of the old ideas conceded that perhaps the stone
objects were man's earliest tools. But they still maintained that the world was at most some six thousand
years old. The idea of great antiquity was abhorrent

to them, because it contradicted the words of the Bible.

The evidence mounted, however.

In 1715 a London pharmacist named Conyers dug up some fossilized bones in Gray's Inn Lane. They seemed to be elephants' bones—and lying among them was a stone axe. What was an elephant doing in England? They lived only in places like India and Africa. Conyers said that at some time in the past elephants had evidently been native to the British Isles, and that ancient Britons had hunted them with weapons of stone.

The scoffers said no: that the elephant was one that the Romans had brought with them when they invaded Britain in the time of Emperor Claudius. No one could easily accept the disturbing idea that exotic tropical creatures like elephants had ever roamed the forests of England.

Other curious deposits of bones came to light elsewhere in Europe—extinct creatures, giant bears and rhinoceroses and several types of elephants. Obviously Europe had been populated by many strange animals in the days before the Deluge. Quite often, axes and spear points were found associated with these remains. In 1790, an Englishman named John Frere, whose hobby was archaeological excavation, found flint axes and fossil bones in Suffolk, England. Frere wrote that the axes were "weapons of war, fabricated and used by a people who had not the use of metals." Near the axes, he declared, were "some extraordinary bones, particularly a jawbone of enormous size, of some unknown animal." He added, "The situation in which these weapons were found may tempt us to refer them to a very remote period indeed; even beyond that of the present world."

*Even beyond that of the present world.* John

20 Frere's seven words opened a gateway into an un-
imaginable, inconceivable epoch of lost yesterdays
when rugged men armed only with weapons of stone
had hunted bizarre beasts of giant size. Repeated
investigations in France, England, and Germany
early in the nineteenth century supported this view.
Archbishop Ussher's six-thousand-year chronology
was tottering under the repeated impact of new discoveries. Explanations grew more ingenious, so that
the literal Biblical text could be preserved. A vast
mound of elaborate theory was heaped up in the
hope of burying the simple idea that mankind and
the world itself might be much more ancient than
Archbishop Ussher thought.

By the middle of the nineteenth century, most
scientists had arrived at a new picture of the past.
Geologists, studying the layers of different minerals
in the earth, showed how old the world really was:
millions, possibly billions of years. It now was clear
that many types of animals had come into being,
endured for incredibly long spans of time, and then
died out. The bones of the giant reptiles known as
dinosaurs had been identified now, and those of
numerous other extinct beasts.

Educated people felt uncomfortable about the new
ideas, but slowly accepted them. They still found it
hard to agree that man himself was really ancient.
The words of the Bible were too powerful to dis-
pute: that on the sixth day of Creation, after all else
was done, the Lord said, "Let us make man in our
image, after our likeness: and let them have dominion over the fish of the sea, and over the fowl of the
air, and over the cattle, and over all the earth, and
over every creeping thing that creepeth upon the
earth."

The men studying the stone axes and the fossil
bones realized that the real picture had to be other-

wise. They knew that man had lived in Europe at the same time as the elephants and giant bears—for there were his axes, embedded in the bones of the long-extinct creatures. Occasionally a human skeleton would also come to light, with flint tools nearby. It was apparent to a very few scholars that man was of great antiquity and had undergone a lengthy development before reaching his present level of culture.

One of those scholars was a Dane named Christian Jürgensen Thomsen, curator of the National Museum at Copenhagen. Thomsen, born in 1788, was the eldest son of a wealthy merchant and shipowner, but showed little interest in following his father's prosperous career. Instead, he devoted his time from boyhood on to coin collecting, and then to collecting other things—such as relics of the ancient past. When a group of Danish antiquarians looked about for someone to bring order to their huge collection of old swords, stone axes, early pottery, and other curios excavated in Denmark, Thomsen seemed just the man.

Starting in 1816, young Thomsen set about organizing the enormous mass of material. Farmers ploughing their land kept uncovering buried archaeological deposits, and most of these objects found their way to Copenhagen. Patiently Thomsen sorted them out—the stone objects in one place, the pottery in another, the metallic things in another. Then he set up categories within each group: tools, weapons, containers, and the like. A pattern gradually emerged, based partly on common sense and partly on observation. In a booklet published in 1836 Thomsen set forth his theory. He saw man's past as divided into three great ages. First, man had gone through *"the Stone Age,* or the period when weapons and tools were made of stone, wood, bone,

22 and similar materials, and in which metals were known either very little or not at all." This had been followed by *"the Bronze Age,* in which the weapons and cutting tools were made of copper or bronze, and when iron and silver have been either very little or not at all known." Then had come *"the Iron Age,* the third and last period of heathen times, in which iron was used for those objects for which it is particularly suitable, so that it took the place of bronze for those things."

Thomsen's system provided a handy way for classifying the artifacts, or ancient relics, that were now being discovered so frequently. He did not mean to say that there had ever been one particular Bronze Age or Iron Age when all the world was at the same level of culture; obviously not, since at the time Thomsen wrote there were still plenty of Stone Age tribes in far-off parts of the world. He merely set up a sequence of development that he felt each human society must pass through, from stone to bronze to iron. The idea was not new, but no one had set it forth so clearly before Thomsen, nor supported it with so much archaeological evidence.

Of course, Thomsen's categories proved too broad to be very useful. As knowledge expanded, it became necessary to divide his Stone Age into two eras: the Old Stone Age or Paleolithic, in which man had fashioned his tools by chipping them to the proper shape, and the New Stone Age or Neolithic, in which tools were shaped by grinding and polishing them. That distinction was first made in 1865 by Sir John Lubbock, the author of a famous book called *Prehistoric Times.* Before long, as we will see, further subdivisions were needed for the precise identification of ancient relics.

A French customs official named Jacques Boucher de Crèvecoeur de Perthes provided much of the evidence on which these new classifications were based. Boucher de Perthes—as he was usually known —was born in the same year as Thomsen, 1788. His father, a government official, was a man of literary and scientific interests, and the boy grew up, as he said, "accustomed from childhood to listen to talk of fossils."

In 1825, when his father retired, Boucher de Perthes became customs director at the town of Abbeville in northern France. The job made little demand on his time and energy, and he was able to undertake a careful scientific study of the local geological structures. While examining a gravel pit just outside of town, he came upon pieces of flint that appeared to have been chipped by human hands into a useful shape. Possibly the shape of these flints was the result of accidental breakage, and only coincidentally looked like human work. In 1832, though, he found an unmistakably man-made stone axe, rounded at one end to fit the hand, chipped to a point at the other. Now Boucher de Perthes became convinced that Abbeville had been occupied by Stone Age man.

Further digging gave him an extensive collection of axes, knives, awls, spear points, and scrapers of stone, along with the animal bones that were usually found associated with such artifacts. When he tried to assert the great age of these relics, however, he met with mockery and scorn. The dead hand of Archbishop Ussher still lay heavily on Europe. "They did not discuss my facts, they did not even take the trouble to deny them," Boucher de Perthes lamented. "They disregarded them."

A Dr. Rigollet of Amiens, one of Boucher de Perthes' most sarcastic detractors, decided to disprove the customs official's findings by conducting some investigations of his own. Rigollet dug at the

24    gravel pit at Abbeville, and was dismayed to turn up more hand axes, in company with the bones of elephants, hippopotamuses, and rhinoceroses. The results were the same when he excavated at the nearby sites of St.-Acheul and St. Rocheles Amiens. In 1854, Rigollet published his excavation report, admitting the truth of Boucher de Perthes' findings. But most French scientists remained skeptical.

Across the Channel in England, the attitude was more sympathetic. In 1858 a schoolmaster named William Pengelly made a discovery that seemed to confirm Boucher de Perthes' notions of the antiquity of man: a cave in Devon on whose floor "lay a sheet of stalagmite from three to eight inches thick having within it and on it relics of lion, hyena, bear, mammoth, rhinoceros, and reindeer." Below that level Pengelly found chipped flint tools.

Pengelly's find led a group of important British geologists and antiquarians to go to France to inspect Boucher de Perthes' material. Among them was John Evans, one of the leading archaeologists of the time. Evans, as he set out, had some doubts. He wrote, "Think of their finding flint axes and arrowheads at Abbeville in conjunction with the bones of elephants forty feet below the surface in a bed of drift. In this bone cave in Devon now being excavated . . . they say they have found flint arrowheads among the bones and the same is reported of a cave in Sicily. I can hardly believe it. It will make my ancient Britons quite modern if man is carried back in England to the days when elephants, rhinoceroses, hippopotamuses and tigers were also inhabitants of the country."

Boucher de Perthes proudly displayed his collection of flint weapons and fossil bones. Then he took his visitors to see the gravel pits themselves. Evans wrote, "Sure enough, the edge of an axe was visible in an entirely undisturbed bed of gravel and eleven feet from the surface. We had a photographer with us to take a view of it so as to corroborate our testimony."

At several meetings of scientists in the summer of 1859, Evans and others gave public backing to Boucher de Perthes' work. Even the skeptics surrendered. The deathblow had been delivered to the notion that the world was born in 4004 B.C. Boucher de Perthes had, as John Evans said, "established beyond doubt that in a period of antiquity remote beyond any of which we have hitherto found traces, this portion of the globe was peopled by man."

The foundations of a science had been laid. Now, working with old bones and pieces of chipped flint, the scientists began the seemingly impossible job of reconstructing the vanished history of prehistoric man.

# 2
# FROM
# THE CAVES
# OF
# FRANCE

A road was under repair near the sleepy French village of Aurignac, in the northern foothills of the Pyrenees. The time was the summer of 1852. Winter's heavy rains had gouged ruts and craters in the un-paved road, and now the workmen were gathering stones to stop up the holes. One man, thinking he saw a usable stone lying in a rabbit hole by the side of the road, stooped to pull it out. He was startled to find that he had grasped a human bone.

The road-menders hastily dug around the rabbit hole and found the entrance to a cave in the hillside. Within lay a grisly sight: seventeen human skeletons, with some scattered tools of flint and whittled bone. The village elders conferred and decided that the workmen had stumbled upon a burial place of Roman times, or perhaps a cemetery of one of the Celtic tribes that had lived in France just before the

28   time of Christ. The seventeen skeletons were given a proper Christian burial in the churchyard at Aurignac, and the discovery was generally forgotten. But for the persistence of a tireless French archaeologist, it might have remained forgotten forever.

The archaeologist was Édouard Lartet, a lawyer who had become interested in the ancient world after reading a book on fossil animals. In 1834, at the age of thirty-three, Lartet conducted some excavations near his home and made such exciting fossil discoveries that he abandoned his law practice on the spot to concentrate on excavations. Between 1836 and 1850 he made a number of major finds, chiefly the bones of fossil apes that we now believe may have been among the earliest ancestors of mankind. Though his own work was concerned chiefly with animal remains, Lartet naturally kept abreast of the discoveries of prehistoric human artifacts by such men as Boucher de Perthes. Lartet, too, believed in the idea of the antiquity of man. It troubled him that there was so little in the way of human skeletal evidence—plenty of chipped flint tools, but hardly any fossil bones of prehistoric man.

In 1859, Lartet chanced to learn of the cave of the seventeen skeletons that had been entered at Aurignac seven years earlier. It struck him that the skeletons might be of great age, and he hurried to Aurignac. Unhappily, he could not view the skeletons. They now rested in the holy soil of the churchyard, and the priests refused to allow them to be disturbed. Lartet had to be content with examining the artifacts of stone and bone that had been found with them.

He recognized them as dating from what was then called the Age of Polished Stone, now termed the New Stone Age or Neolithic—which made them as old as the Pyramids of Egypt, possibly even older.

Hurriedly Lartet went to the cave and began to excavate. The topmost layer of soil contained more relics of the relatively recent Age of Polished Stone. In any undisturbed deposit of relics, the newest material will obviously be at the top of the heap. Digging downward, Lartet found in the lower layers an assortment of Old Stone Age remains: crude chipped flint tools, implements of bone and ivory, and the fossilized bones of extinct animals such as the woolly mammoth and the woolly rhinoceros.

These shaggy beasts, scientists had discovered not long before, had lived in Europe at a time when France had had an arctic climate. How long ago that had been, no one was prepared to say; but Lartet's finds at Aurignac clearly showed that man, the tool-making animal, had lived in France at the time of the Ice Age, hunting the woolly beasts. Lartet needed more proof, though.

At this time, amateur archaeologists were beginning to root about in caves all over France, gathering the flint tools that were so surprisingly easy to find. Since there was no system to their explorations, these well-meaning diggers did a great deal of harm by disturbing the ancient layers, making it impossible to arrive at the relative ages of the deposits at any one site. But they also served the useful purpose of bringing key locations to the attention of the professional scientists. In 1863, one of these collectors read Lartet's book on the Aurignac cave and sent him a selection of flints and bones that he had found in the district known as the Dordogne, in southwest France. They had come, he wrote, from the rock shelters of Les Éyzies. Lartet at once turned his attention there.

He was joined by his English friend Henry Christy, a banker who had inherited a vast fortune. Bored with the making of even more money, Christy had

30    traveled widely, studying the customs of primitive communities in many parts of the world and forming a magnificent collection of native handicrafts. Such a man could not resist the exciting new field of prehistoric studies, and he offered to provide financial backing for Lartet's work. Together they planned a careful level-by-level exploration of the district around Les Éyzies. Their goal was to work out the proper sequence of types of stone tools, from the earliest to the most recent, and match them with the right animal types of each era.

A rock shelter is not a true cave, but simply an overhanging ledge with a huddling-place beneath. The swift-running Vézère River had carved a series of such rock shelters out of the soft limestone cliffs along its banks. An initial survey showed Lartet and Christy that prehistoric men had camped in virtually all of the rock shelters at some time, leaving discarded tools and the bones of slaughtered animals behind to be buried in the soil by the forces of nature. Using the village of Les Éyzies as their base, the archaeologists began to work their way methodically up the river from shelter to shelter.

Stone tools of familiar types came to light at once. Then, four hundred yards up the river at a place called Laugerie Haute, they made their first significant new discoveries. Here the overhanging ledge had crashed down long ago, walling up the front of the shelter and creating a natural cave. Prehistoric man had evidently found it an inviting place, for it had been occupied long enough to pile up an accumulation of human debris fourteen feet thick. Cutting down through this heap of bones, shells, flints, ashes, charcoal, and other refuse, Lartet and Christy were easily able to see the layers of wind-blown sand and rain-swept gravel that told of the years when no one had lived there. The refuse heap was like a many-layered sandwich: the discarded trash of each human era alternated with its covering level of sand and gravel.

The upper layer yielded finely worked stone blades. Bones of reindeer and wild horses were associated with these flints. Below was a layer of less elegant stone tools, which Lartet recognized as similar in style to the ones he had found at Aurignac. These, again, were found with such Ice Age fossils as the woolly mammoth and rhinoceros. Even cruder tools were uncovered in the third layer from the top. The first season's work thus yielded the relics of three prehistoric cultures. They must have flourished at widely separated times, since the local animal life had changed from era to era. Steady refinement in the art of chipping stone tools could be observed in the sequence.

Moving up the valley, Lartet and Christy dug at the rock shelter of La Madeleine and found in the top layer carefully fashioned artifacts in a style different from that of the top layer at Laugerie Haute. Obviously these were the work of some culture later than any that had occupied the other cave. Still further up the river, at the village of Le Moustier, the archaeologists came upon a sequence that moved in the opposite direction. Here, the uppermost level matched the *lowest* level of Laugerie Haute. Below that, under a thick sterile layer marking a time when the rock shelter had been abandoned, were tools of a strikingly different sort from any that had been found earlier—not only cruder in technique, but formed in an entirely distinctive manner. Whereas the tools in the higher levels had been made out of chips struck from large flint cores, these objects were the large cores themselves, roughly shaped for their function. Lartet and Christy realized that they had come upon the de-

32    posits of an earlier, more primitive people. The rock
shelter at Le Moustier gave them one more thrill:
below the levels of the core tools, they found even
more crude hand axes of the types found at Abbeville
and St.-Acheul by Boucher de Perthes and Dr.
Rigollet.

It was a brilliant, breathtaking archaeological
achievement. Lartet and Christy had done exactly
what they had set out to do. They had identified a
sequence of seven types of stone tools, from the early
and clumsy ones of the Abbeville and St.-Acheul
styles to the delicate, graceful ones of La Madeleine.
They had tied together the work of all other investigators, and they had linked certain species of extinct animals to definite styles of axes and spear
points. Out of nothing more glamorous than pieces
of chipped stone, the two investigators had spun an
epic of slow but steady human progress over what
must have been many thousands of years.

In April 1865, at the height of his scientific fame,
Henry Christy caught a severe cold while exploring
a cave in Belgium. It developed into pneumonia, and
by the beginning of May he was dead, only fifty-four
years old. His will left a good part of his fortune to
finance Lartet's continued work. Accompanied now
only by his twenty-four-year-old son Louis, Édouard
Lartet returned to the rock shelters of the Dordogne.

Though by now Lartet had amassed a collection of
thousands of flint tools, he had not yet come upon
any human skeletal remains. The endless rows of
gray flints, while they were exciting enough to anyone capable of reading their story, lacked the magic
that could stir wide public enthusiasm. Only if the
toolmakers themselves were uncovered would that
shadowy figure, prehistoric man, step into the light.

Some ancient skeletons had already been discovered. The most famous of these was the "Red

Lady of Paviland," found in 1823 by an English clergyman, William Buckland. The Red Lady was no lady at all, but the skeleton of a young man, dyed red with ocher. At that time, though, the idea of man's antiquity was not generally recognized. Although the Red Lady's skeleton had been accompanied by flint tools, Buckland himself insisted that "she" dated back only to the time of Christ. Not for forty more years would anyone realize that the Red Lady had been buried five to ten thousand years ago.

A much more startling human relic was discovered in 1856 at a limestone quarry in the valley of Neanderthal, near Düsseldorf, Germany. This was a skull, strangely brutish in form, with a sloping forehead out of which bulged an enormous ridge above the brows. The walls of the skull were much thicker than those of ordinary men. Thighbones found near the skull were so massive that they scarcely seemed human at all.

The Neanderthal bones reached scientific attention at a meeting in Bonn in 1857. Though a German scientist hailed them as "the most ancient memorial of the early inhabitants of Europe," they attracted no international curiosity until 1861. Then, an English geologist named George Busk translated the German scientific report and gave a lecture on Neanderthal man. He said he had "no doubt of the enormous antiquity" of the Neanderthal bones, and pointed out that the shape of the skull approached "that of some of the higher apes."

Charles Darwin's theory of evolution had been made public two years earlier. Darwin had claimed that living things evolve—change—over the course of time, responding to the pressure of their environment and gradually altering their forms. Darwin's theory seemed to contradict the Biblical idea of a single time of Creation when all things had been

*34* given a lasting form. Therefore it was bitterly attacked by orthodox religion, despite the wealth of proofs with which Darwin bolstered his claims. Now here was Neanderthal man, seemingly the evidence that man himself had evolved from a more primitive form.

At first, many authorities tried to dismiss the Neanderthal skull as that of a deformed individual whose skeleton had been distorted by some dreadful disease. As other skulls of the same type were discovered, however, it became more difficult to argue that they all represented the same kind of affliction. Rather, it became obvious that a strange type of human being once had lived in Europe, with thick bones, a receding forehead, scarcely any chin at all, and huge eyes topped by protruding brow ridges. A

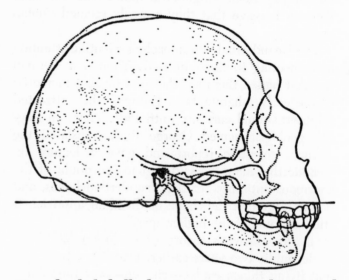

*Neanderthal skull, showing projecting brows and jaw. Modern human skull is outlined with dotted line for comparison.*

real understanding of Neanderthal man's place in the evolutionary scheme still was far in the future while Édouard Lartet excavated along the Vézère.

Lartet still hoped to find the actual skeletons of the ancient toolmakers. As we have seen, there had been one such discovery at Aurignac in 1852, but those skeletons had been whisked off into the sanctuary of the churchyard before any scientist could examine them. There had to be some other burial in the limestone cliffs, Lartet was convinced.

In 1868, during the course of railway construction at Les Éyzies, workmen found ancient relics in the rock shelter of Cro-Magnon, some two hundred yards from the village. Their spades turned up the customary animal bones and flint tools, by now such commonplace items at Les Éyzies that they caused no stir whatever. But there also appeared to be human bones buried against the face of the cliff.

Quickly, young Louis Lartet arrived and took charge of the excavation. He uncovered five human skeletons. They were accompanied by implements of the same type as those found at Aurignac.

A prehistoric tragedy had occurred at Cro-Magnon. Three men, a woman, and a child had been murdered there, the woman by a powerful blow to the skull. About them lay necklaces of pierced shells, the perforated teeth of animals, ivory pendants—all the pathetic finery of the murdered people. The Lartets, father and son, at last could stare across the ages at the actual remains of prehistoric man.

The Cro-Magnon skeletons were nothing at all like the grotesque Neanderthal bones. Far from being brutish and primitive in form, these people had been strikingly handsome, fully human, physically superior to most human beings of modern times. The men were well over six feet in height. They had had high

# THE OLD STONE AGE:
# LOWER PALEOLITHIC PERIOD

*Duration: 1,000,000 years or more. All dates on chronological charts are approxima*

**FIRST GLACIERS**

| | | |
|---|---|---|
| **CHELLEAN or ABBEVILLEAN CULTURE** | Several hundreds of thousands of years before 350,000 B.C. | Warm and tropical. Jungle growth. Elephants, tigers, hippopotamus |

**SECOND GLACIERS: duration about 60,000 years**

| | | |
|---|---|---|
| **ACHEULIAN and CLACTONIAN CULTURES** | 350,000 – 250,000 B.C. | Warm period. |

**THIRD GLACIERS: duration about 50,000 years**

| | | |
|---|---|---|
| **MOUSTERIAN CULTURE** | .180,000 – 130,000 B.C. | Warm period. |
| **MOUSTERIAN CULTURE** continues | 130,000 – 30,000 B.C. | Cool period during and after glaciers Wooly mammoth and rhinoceros, reindeer cave bears and lions. |

**FOURTH GLACIERS: duration about 60,000 years**

As the weather grows warmer . . .

*Lower Paleolithic dates are very approximate.*

||||||||||||||||||||||||||||||||||||||||||||||||||||||||||||||||||||||||||||||||||||||||||||||||||||||||||||||||||||||||||||||

*Early men, perhaps Heidelberg man,* Crude stone hand axes

||||||||||||||||||||||||||||||||||||||||||||||||||||||||||||||||||||||||||||||||||||||||||||||||||||||||||||||||||||||||||||||

*Acheulians,* first *Homo sapiens* people. Hand axes, flint tools, scrapers.
Evidence of use of fire. Left Europe when the glaciers returned.

*Clactonians,* Neanderthal type skulls. Co-existed with Acheulians,
but remained in Europe.

||||||||||||||||||||||||||||||||||||||||||||||||||||||||||||||||||||||||||||||||||||||||||||||||||||||||||||||||||||||||||||||

*Neanderthal man* dominant in Europe, persisting through glacial period.

*Fontechévade people, Homo sapiens* type, appear in Europe only during warm period.

*Neanderthal man.* Hand axes and scrapers, knives, awls and points of stone.
Tools with retouched edges. First burials indicate belief in afterlife.

||||||||||||||||||||||||||||||||||||||||||||||||||||||||||||||||||||||||||||||||||||||||||||||||||||||||||||||||||||||||||||||

*Cro-Magnon man,* a *Homo sapiens* type,
returns to Europe, bringing the new cultures of the Upper Paleolithic
Period. Neanderthal man disappears forever.

38    foreheads, prominent cheekbones, firm chins. Tall, powerful, splendidly shaped, these ancestral figures seemed like titans out of some forgotten golden age of mankind.

Before his death in 1871, Lartet published his system of classification of the epochs of the Old Stone Age. It summed up a lifetime of superb work. Geologists had shown that there had been great changes in the European climate over the past several hundred thousand years. (Scientists now were thinking in terms of hundreds of thousands of years, although many diehards still defended Archbishop Ussher's timetable of Creation.) Long ago, it was known, Europe had had a tropical climate. Then had come an era of extremely cold weather, followed by a gradual warming, another Ice Age, and another thaw—possibly three or four Ice Ages in all. (Scientists believe today that there were four.) Lartet's excavations had produced the bones of animals of differing climates in Europe, showing that the geological theories were right. Now he linked the sequence of stone tools to the sequence of climatic changes and the sequence of animal life.

Lartet's system began with a Hippopotamus Age, when Europe had been inhabited by beasts of a sort now found in Africa, such as the elephant and hippopotamus. The extremely crude tools found at St.-Acheul and Abbeville belonged to this epoch. It was followed by the Mammoth Age, a frigid era when glaciers descended on Europe and the fur-covered beasts had thrived: the woolly mammoth and rhinoceros, the cave bear, the bison. The implements from the middle level at Le Moustier dated from that time. This was the era of Neanderthal man. Finally, as the weather grew warm again, the woolly beasts died out and were replaced by the reindeer, the wild horse, and other modern animals. Lartet called this the Reindeer Age: an era when men still lived in caves and rock shelters, but were making rapid strides in the art of fashioning tools. The implements from Aurignac, Laugerie Haute, and La Madeleine showed successive stages of this Reindeer Age, and the noble looking men from Cro-Magnon were representatives of its people.

It was a valuable system as far as it went. But its view of Old Stone Age culture was not precise enough to admit the new evidence constantly being discovered. It failed to take into account the fact that there had been four major periods of extreme cold, alternating with warmer eras, or that woolly mammoths had actually existed well into Lartet's Reindeer Age. The idea of linking tool types to animal types was useful, but did not permit sufficient flexibility. After Lartet's death, his system was revised.

The man responsible for the revisions was Louis de Mortillet, a Frenchman who had studied engineering and geology before being exiled from his homeland for political reasons. Mortillet lived in Switzerland and earned his living as an engineer, planning and supervising excavations for railway roadbeds. In the course of this work many fossils turned up, and Mortillet grew interested in paleontology—the study of fossil bones. He became such an expert in the field that he left engineering entirely to become a paleontologist. Mortillet returned to France in 1863 after sixteen years of exile, and five years later became director of the new Museum of Prehistory in Paris. Recognizing the faults of Lartet's system of classification, he soon began to develop his own. He knew that it was a mistake to name the epochs after animal life, since the range of animals is governed by the weather in a particular locality,

*40*  whereas the style of stone tools evidently was the same all over Europe at any one time. So he chose the simple method of naming each epoch after a site where its relics were discovered.

He renamed the Hippopotamus Age the Chellean, after the town of Chelles, near Paris, where crude hand axes had been found. He divided the Mammoth Age into the Mousterian, after the cave of Le Moustier, and the Aurignacian, from the cave at Aurignac. The Reindeer Age became the Solutrean and the Magdalenian, named for sites at Solutré in eastern France and La Madeleine in the Dordogne. The Solutrean relics were like those found in the top layer at Laugerie Haute; Mortillet gave the period that name to avoid confusion with other discoveries made at a place called Laugerie Basse.

Over the next twenty years Mortillet tinkered with his classifications as new evidence emerged. He added the Acheulian Period as a transition from the Chellean to the Mousterian, naming it for Dr. Rigollet's site at St.-Acheul. He decided to drop the Aurignacian, then restored it. He introduced a new period called the pre-Chellean or Thenaisian at the beginning of his sequence. At the time of his death in 1898 Mortillet was the dominant figure in European archaeology, a revered and respected teacher whose ideas had won universal acclaim.

Mortillet's classification is still in use, with some slight modifications. The Aurignacian has been split into three periods, to account for certain local variations in style. The Chellean is now usually called the Abbevillean, to give credit to the site of the pioneer Boucher de Perthes. Most important, the system is now recognized as having meaning only for western Europe, not as Mortillet thought, for the entire world. Other sets of names have been devised to

show the pattern of tool development elsewhere. Yet,
because it was the first of its kind, the Mortillet
system is still acclaimed as an invaluable guide. It
serves as a beacon that illuminates the darkness of
prehistory.

# 3
# THE
# MORNING
# OF
# MANKIND

A century has passed since the time of the pioneers, Boucher de Perthes and Édouard Lartet, Henry Christy and Louis de Mortillet. They moved uncertainly through unknown realms, but today a clear and detailed picture of man's development has emerged. A host of discoveries showed the story: fossil bones, hordes of discarded tools, glorious paintings on the walls of caves, cemeteries rich with the artifacts of ancient man. Though prehistory still holds many puzzles, the general pattern of events is no longer open to serious challenge.

Perhaps the most unsettling discovery of all was the revelation that other species of men once walked the earth. Today, all human beings belong to the same species, which bears the not very humble scientific name of *Homo sapiens,* "man the wise." *Homo sapiens* is divided into a number of races,

44 which differ from one another in such things as skin color and body structure. Although these differences may appear on the surface to be very great, they are actually minor compared with those that distinguish us from our early ancestors.

We are not yet sure where the first manlike creatures evolved, but the latest evidence seems to point toward Africa. Certain fossil apes from Africa appear to belong on our family tree, such as *Proconsul*, who lived forty million years ago, and *Kenyapithecus*, who dates back fourteen million years. The fossil record has large gaps in it, and the next group of manlike creatures can be traced back only two million years. They are the australopithecines— various species of apes who stood about four feet high and walked on their hind legs alone. That left their hands free for the manufacture and use of tools. Perhaps it was these australopithecines who first began to bang and pound rocks into useful shapes.

So many types of manlike fossils have been found in Africa in the past few years that it is still difficult to arrive at a logical sequence of evolutionary events there. It does seem that the little australopithecines gradually gave way to taller upright-walking creatures with bigger brains and flatter faces. Slowly these men of the dawn spread to other continents, and evolution continued to work its effects on them as thousands of years passed.

In 1891, a Dutch surgeon on the island of Java discovered the skull of a man who had lived half a million years ago. The following year, a thighbone of the same species was unearthed a few yards away. The fossil was undoubtedly human, though the skull was thick and strange. The discoverer named his find *Pithecanthropus erectus*, "ape-man that walks upright." The Javan man had a brain smaller than that of modern man but larger than that of a gorilla or a chimpanzee. Later, an equally primitive type of man was discovered in China, and still later a similar form in Africa.

No such ape-man fossils have ever been found in Europe. But in 1907 a strange jawbone was discovered by workmen digging in a sandpit near Heidelberg, Germany. Extremely thick and heavy and lacking any trace of a chin, the jawbone might well have been that of some big ape—except that it had a full set of teeth, and the teeth were definitely human in shape and arrangement. Heidelberg man, who seems to have lived half a million years ago, is still unknown but for that single jawbone. Yet scientists think that men of this type were the manufacturers of the crude Chellean-Abbevillean hand axes.

The use of tools is not exclusively a human trait. A chimpanzee may pick up a handy stick and use it to knock down a bunch of bananas lying beyond his reach, for example. In just the same way, the earliest men must have made use of handy chunks of rock to split open a coconut, kill an animal, or divide up a piece of meat.

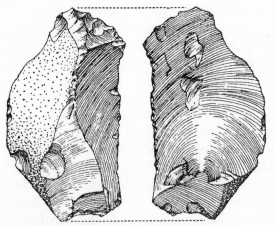

*Chellean hand axes.*

*46*    From the use of tools to the *manufacture* of tools is a colossal leap. After hundreds of thousands of years of making do with any rock that might be available, men began shaping stones to suit their needs. Some tribal genius saw how it could be done, and the word spread. Probably the idea was developed separately in many places.

The hard, shiny stone known as flint eventually established itself as the material most suited for toolmaking. When a flint is struck properly, it fractures, leaving a sharp edge along the line of the break. Early men in Africa chipped pebbles of lava or quartz into choppers, but in time flint won universal favor.

The Chellean-Abbevillean hand axes, the proudest achievement of mankind half a million years ago, are simple pear-shaped tools three to six inches long, round at one end, pointed at the other. With great intellectual effort, no doubt, the Abbevilleans struck one rock against another until they achieved the desired triangular form. Since we have no complete human skeletons from this period, we can only guess at how well adapted their hands and fingers were for such taxing work. Perhaps it was a real challenge for clumsy Abbevillean fingers to hold the flint in place. Certainly Abbevillean minds were not very dynamic, since hundreds of thousands of years passed with no change in the method of making hand axes; one generation after another placidly pounded out tools exactly as they had been fashioned ages ago.

By the time man had learned to make even these simple tools, he had already been driven out of Europe at least once by a glacial period. Along with the warm-weather beasts, the elephant and the hippopotamus, he retreated to Africa when the freeze began, drifting northward again as the weather relented. The Abbevillean Period was a time of almost tropical warmth in Europe, and man probably hunted the big creatures of the torrid jungles. The hand axe served as an all-purpose tool, a combined hatchet, saw, knife, pick, and scraper. A strong blow with the business end could split an enemy's skull or kill a fairly large animal. Hand axes could not be used for hunting elephants, of course; but if the Abbevilleans came upon a lone elephant they might try to stampede it over a cliff, and then they could use their tools to cut it up for a feast. The axe was possibly employed to hack limbs from trees to use as clubs, to dress hides as clothing, or to split wood for burning. These are all guesses, naturally. We know nothing about the culture of Abbevillean man except the shape of his hand axes.

Slowly, improvements in hand-axe design were made—enough to lead prehistorians to distinguish a new cultural period, the Acheulian. A second Ice Age had occurred, lasting sixty thousand years, to divide this phase from the Abbevillean. Acheulian axes are flatter and more evenly flaked than Abbevillean ones. They have sharp, straight cutting edges. They are still clumsy tools, though, not good for more than the simplest uses. Cutting and chopping were the limits of their functions.

We know of a few fossil human remains from the Acheulian Period. They date from the warm epoch about three hundred thousand years ago, between the second Ice Age and the third. One of these relics —two fragments of a skull found in 1935 in Swanscombe, England—indicates that Acheulian man was well along the evolutionary road toward the form of modern man, *Homo sapiens*.

It appears that the human stock had already split into its two great evolutionary lines. One was the *Homo sapiens* line. The other was a line more closely derived from the ape-men of Java, with their thick

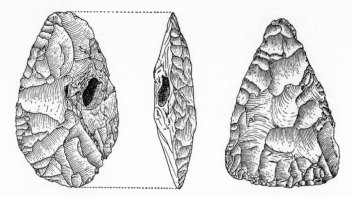

*Acheulian flint tools.*

bones, receding chins, and bulging brows. This other line, which is now extinct, culminated eventually in Neanderthal man.

The evidence for this view is still sketchy. It consists of just a few bits of fossilized bone and some hand axes. But gradually new research is making the pattern clear. Not only were there two diverging species of human beings, but each had its own way of making tools and each preferred a different sort of weather.

About two hundred and fifty thousand years ago a third Ice Age began to engulf Europe. The Acheulians—the *Homo sapiens* line—headed for warmer lands in a slow migration that probably lasted thousands of years. They left Europe to a rival cultural group that began to emerge as the weather cooled. These were the Clactonians, named for Clacton, the English town where their relics first were found. Archaeologists think that the Clactonians were of that separate stock that developed into Neanderthal man, and thus were not our ancestors at all.

All we know about the Clactonians is that they did

not use heavy hand axes. Rather, their tools were
fashioned from slender flakes chipped off flint cores
—the sort of flakes that hand-axe people threw away.
Clactonian tools were apparently meant to serve as
skinning-knives and hide-scrapers, which would be
useful in a cold climate where fur clothing was a
necessity.

The Acheulians did not entirely abandon Europe
during this third Ice Age. Though they withdrew
from England, France, and Germany, Acheulian people remained in the Mediterranean region. Those
who stayed adapted to the colder weather. They
learned how to make scrapers of flint as well as their
traditional hand axes, so we can guess that they, too,
were using animal hides for clothing. And, since we
have found charcoal hearths in Acheulian sites, we
know that they had fire as well as furs.

For thousands of years, Acheulians and Clactonians occupied Europe simultaneously. We can be
fairly sure that they were separate cultures, and quite
probably there was occasional warfare whenever
their hunting grounds overlapped. As we have noted,
it also seems likely that the differences between them
were not merely in styles of tools; they were separate
species of mankind, much less similar to one another
than, say, Negroes and Chinese are today.

Why mankind should have taken two evolutionary
paths is anyone's guess. But the record of the fossils
shows that that is what happened. The "cold-
weather" Clactonian people, with their flake tools
and fur clothes, evolved toward the thick-boned,
chinless, big-browed Neanderthal type. The "warm-
weather" Acheulian people, wielders of hand axes,
evolved toward a kind of man with slender bones, a
high-vaulted skull, and a jutting chin.

When the third Ice Age ended, the ancestors of
modern man returned once again. This was open to

50     scientific question for a long time, but a significant discovery made in 1937 provided the first evidence of the presence of *Homo sapiens* in Europe between the third and fourth Ice Ages. A cave in the valley of Fontéchevade, in west-central France, held Mousterian (Neanderthal) deposits of the fourth Ice Age. Below them—that is, in an earlier deposit— were the bones of the tropical rhinoceros of the pre- vious warm period. Fossil human remains were eventually found in these pre-Mousterian levels— and they were *Homo sapiens*. Lying with them were more bones of tropical mammals, and flint tools of a kind termed Tayacian.

So the Fontéchevade people and the Neanderthals shared Europe between the third and fourth Ice Ages, just as the Acheulians and the Clactonians did between the second and the third. The Fontéchevade people lived in France about one hundred and eighty thousand years ago and thrived in the warm weather.

*Mousterian tools with retouched edges.*

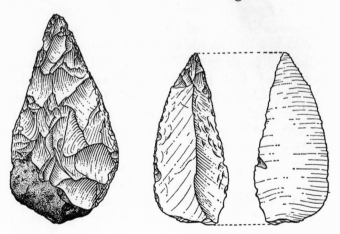

But, like their Acheulian ancestors, they abandoned
Europe when the next Ice Age arrived, withdrawing
to Asia and Africa and leaving Europe to the tougher
folk of the other species.

This was the great era of Neanderthal man, beginning about a hundred and thirty thousand years ago
and lasting close to a hundred thousand years. The
type of tool that Mortillet called Mousterian was the

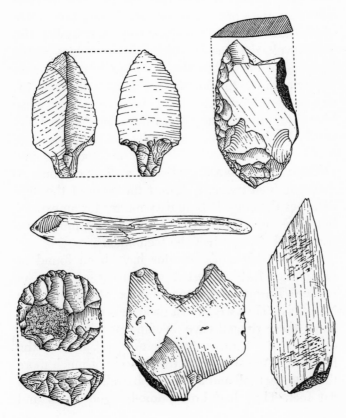

52 work of Neanderthal man. ("Mousterian" is the name applied to the culture, "Neanderthal" the name given to the fossil skeletal type.) Mousterian tools, which seem to have developed out of the Clactonian ones, came in many varieties. The Neanderthals used hand axes, but did not make them in the Abbevillean-Acheulian way. Instead of chopping big cores of flint down to size, they knocked medium-big pieces off larger cores and then worked them carefully.

The Mousterian culture had an elaborate tool kit far surpassing anything that had come before. There were knives and awls, scrapers and weapon points, each designed for its special function. That indicates how much more complex the Neanderthal people were than their predecessors. They developed a technique that we call "retouching" to perfect their tools. This involved detaching tiny flakes or chips along the edge of the tool to provide a keener cutting surface. Because retouched flint tools are still made by modern-day Stone Age tribes, we have a good idea how these Mousterian blades must have been fashioned. Modern craftsmen usually hold the piece of flint in the left hand and apply a retouching implement made from an antler or a sliver of bone. A quick, sudden pressure against the edge of the flint detaches the chip. It is an easy matter for an expert; but thousands of years of experimentation must have been needed to perfect the technique.

Neanderthal man's remains have been found at more than forty different sites, most of them in western Europe but some in Asia Minor and the Near East. Thus we have a good deal of information about these rugged cave-dwelling people who were dominant in Europe just before and during the fourth Ice Age. We know they stood not much more than five feet tall and had deep, barrellike chests and flat feet. They had broad, low-bridged noses and forward-jutting, muzzlelike mouths. Their foreheads sloped steeply backward, and they had only rounded snubs where we have chins. Though they were coarse and apelike in appearance, we have no right to sneer at their intelligence, for the average Neanderthal brain was bigger than that of the average modern man. No doubt they were as bright as our own ancestors were. The wide variety of Mousterian tools indicates as much.

What little we know about Neanderthal man's way of life indicates that he was far from being an ape. He had some civilized traits. He cared for the elderly and ailing, for example; many of the Neanderthal fossils that have been discovered show signs of afflictions that mere beasts would not have tolerated. One was crippled with arthritis and had just two teeth. Someone had cared for the ailing Neanderthal, had supplied him with food that he could chew, and had at last given him a reverent burial. Another Neanderthal whose skeleton was found in Iraq had had a withered right arm, which had been amputated by a surgeon; the man had survived the operation by many years. These instances show a definite humanity. The fact that the Neanderthals buried their dead leads us to suspect that they had some notion of an afterlife. They interred objects with their dead, also. One cave in Germany contained ten bear skulls in niches in the walls, and more bones of bears on a stone platform. Possibly the bear was an object of worship to the Neanderthals.

They were men. In an epoch of fierce cold, they endured and flourished. They were masters of Europe for a thousand centuries—a period so long that the mind refuses to comprehend it.

Then they vanished.

We have no clue to the reasons for their disappearance. The archaeological record in the caves is silent

54 on that score; but each cave tells the same story. Layers of sterile sand cover the Mousterian flake tools. Above are the deposits of a wholly different culture, which we call the Aurignacian, with objects of bone and horn and ivory, carved statuettes, flint tools of many shapes. The squat, thick-bodied Neanderthals are replaced by the towering men of the Cro-Magnon type. We can picture, if we like, some terrible war of conquest, fought from cave to cave against the bleak backdrop of the frozen world. We can imagine Neanderthal blood staining the glacial snow as the invaders—more agile, more intelligent —carried out their campaign of extermination. We can see the last few Neanderthals driven into the barren wasteland, hunted down, starved out, taken as slaves. All this is speculation, of course. But the swiftness of the Neanderthal doom seems to point to a grim massacre.

Though we do not know the details of their downfall, we know approximately when the Neanderthals perished, thanks to an important modern archaeological technique, carbon-14 dating. Carbon-14 is a radioactive element. All living things absorb it at a steady rate while alive. When they die, the intake of C-14 halts, and the accumulated supply begins to break down. The breakdown rate, or "half-life," is known. An elaborate method has been developed for measuring the C-14 content of organic substances, thus revealing how long ago it was that death came. Carbon-14 dating can give a reliable age for material up to about fifty thousand years old, and works best with samples of wood or charcoal.

Charcoal found in the hearth of a Neanderthal camp in an Israeli cave gave a C-14 date of approximately thirty thousand years. A Belgian cave contained Mousterian stone tools in a layer of peat with a C-14 date of thirty-six thousand years. A cave in Iraq occupied by Neanderthals yielded an age of forty-six thousand years for the settlement there. So we know that Neanderthals still survived as recently as thirty thousand years ago, and probably for five or ten thousand years after that. They lasted into the final centuries of the fourth Ice Age. By the time the glaciers melted, they were gone.

What of the conquerors? Who were they? Where did they come from?

We know that the *Homo sapiens* evolutionary line shared Europe with the Neanderthal line for hundreds of thousands of years, but withdrew every time the cold weather settled in. Thus, as we have seen, the Acheulian hand-axe people of the *Homo sapiens* line withdrew when the third Ice Age began, leaving most of Europe to the Clactonian flake-tool people. Then, we think, the ancestors of modern man returned when the weather grew warm. These, the Fontéchevade people, departed again at the outset of the fourth Ice Age. Archaeologists working in Lebanon have discovered what may have been an outpost of *Homo sapiens* of one hundred thousand years ago. There, perhaps, the future world-masters, our ancestors, bided their time while Neanderthal man hunted in glacier-covered Europe.

Then, for the fourth time, the ice began to retreat. It was no sudden thaw, but rather an infinitely slow process that saw the glaciers pulling back by a few hundred feet each year. The winters became less brutal; snowfall was no longer so heavy; spring arrived earlier each year. Roving tribes, seeking new hunting grounds, began to edge northward out of the warm countries. There was no overnight rush into Europe. The invaders moved cautiously, camping for years in the same region, then pressing on-

56 ward. At last they were in France and Germany, the heartland of the Neanderthals. Then came the collision of cultures, and the swift annihilation of one human stock.

Men who are recognizably related to us now were again in command of Europe. The Ice Age had not yet ended, but its worst phase had passed. In the new dawn of mankind came a rush of ideas, a tide of change. It had taken man thousands of weary centuries to move from the Abbevillean type of hand axe to the Acheulian kind. In their hundred thousand years of dominance, the Neanderthals had scarcely progressed at all beyond their beginnings. Now, new phases of culture would emerge every few thousand years, and then every few hundred years, as the pace of progress increased. The coming of the conquerors, thirty thousand years ago, was not the beginning of the story of man, but we see it as the opening of an exciting epoch of development. Those who give names to the eras of mankind set this epoch off from the rest of the Old Stone Age or Paleolithic. They call it the Upper Paleolithic. It lasted only some fifteen thousand years before it was succeeded by an era of even greater change. But the Lower Paleolithic—all that had gone before—had endured for a million years or more.

Man at the outset of the Upper Paleolithic still had a great deal to learn. He knew nothing of farming. He could not build houses. He had no herds of livestock. The use of metals was unknown to him. He had no permanent settlements, but drifted from place to place, following the animals that were his food supply. He was a simple hunter, a savage, a wanderer.

Compared to those who had preceded him, though, he stood at the summit of human accom-

plishment. He had triumphed over the ugly Neanderthals, and had planted his foot firmly on Europe. No
doubt he looked back at the defeated race as con-
temptible brutes, and regarded his own glowing
accomplishments with pride and satisfaction. He
was a *man*, and that was no small thing.

# 4
# THE
# AURIGNACIANS

A statement frequently heard about prehistoric man gives the Cro-Magnon people credit for having replaced the Neanderthals. That is true as far as it goes, but it does not go far enough. The Cro-Magnons—those tall, improbably handsome folk who moved into France some thirty thousand years ago—were the most spectacular looking of the new invaders. But they were not the only ones who came. At least two other physical types of Upper Paleolithic man have been identified since the discovery of the Cro-Magnon skeletons in 1868. Some authorities think that these three types represent separate races of mankind that dwelt in Europe at the close of the fourth Ice Age. A more widely accepted belief is that the differing skeletons represent nothing more than the normal range of bodily variation within any group of human beings.

The Cro-Magnons, as we have seen, were unusu-

# THE OLD STONE AGE:
# UPPER PALEOLITHIC PERIOD

*Duration: about 20,000 years*

| | | |
|---|---|---|
| **CHATELPERRONIAN, AURIGNACIAN, and GRAVETTIAN CULTURES** | 30,000— 25,000 B.C. | Cool climate, Northern Europe covere with ice. Cave animals, wolves, bison, wild horse |
| **SOLUTREAN CULTURE** | 20,000— 15,000 B.C. | Cool period. |
| **MAGDALENIAN CULTURE** | 15,000— 10,000 B.C. | Glaciers recede; Europe continuousl warmer. Pine forests follow birch an willow. Grazing animals go north or di out. |

ally big people, with strong cheekbones and wide
faces. Quite unlike them were the Chancelade people, first identified in 1888 at Chancelade, France.
These were short, stocky men with long arms and
large feet. The Grimaldi people, whose remains were
discovered in 1901 in a cave near Monaco, were even
shorter and quite slender, with some anatomical features that have been called Negroid in appearance.

We can see, then, that the newcomers who took
over Europe at the start of the Upper Paleolithic

*Chatelperronian, Chancelade, Grimaldi people.* Transitional cultures.

*Cro-Magnon man* replaces Neanderthal man in Europe, migrating from East Asia through the Balkans into France.
Fine flint tools, spearpoints. Bone pins and awls. Birth of art: carving in bone, horn, ivory; cave paintings at Lascaux. Magic and religion.

*Gravettian hunters* inhabit steppes of East and Central Europe, move into Western Europe. Sharp gravette knives; pit houses, use of coal. Ivory carving and Venus statuettes; stone graves indicate belief in afterlife.

---

*Solutrean peoples* in Europe. Laurel leaf and willow points, bone tools.

---

*Magdalenian peoples* flourish, develop highest form of Stone Age life, then follow game animals north or disappear.
Long knives, spear points, harpoons, spear-throwers. Very high level of art: carved bone, horn, ivory; sculpture and cave painting as at Altamira.

---

Warm weather changes the hunting life of the cave period. The peoples of the Old Stone Age follow the game north. New transitional cultures begin to develop in their place.

were just about as varied in form as Europeans are today. It is a mistake to think that they all had the striking Cro-Magnon physique.

On the other hand, though they differed among themselves in appearance, all of them were quite distinct from the Neanderthals. They lacked the enormous brow ridges of the other human stock, and their chins were well developed. Many basic features of the skeletal construction also set the invaders off from the Neanderthal type.

62

Like the Neanderthals, they lived by hunting. Their chief prey, when they first entered Europe after their long sojourn in warmer climates, were the shaggy beasts of the Ice Age: the woolly mammoth and the woolly rhinoceros. The woolly mammoth was a type of elephant covered with a thick coat of coarse reddish hair. Its head was topped with an odd hump, its neck was short, its back sloped steeply toward the tail, and its tusks curved inward so much that they often crossed. The woolly rhinoceros, also wrapped in a heavy fur coat, had a long, narrow head from which sprouted two lengthy and formidable horns. These big creatures must have been dangerous foes, and probably it took the combined efforts of a large group of men to slay one.

Lesser animals grazed along the fringes of the retreating sheets of ice: the arctic fox, the arctic hare, the reindeer, and other animals now found only in northern lands. The caves were inhabited by the huge cave bear, the cave lion, the cave leopard, and the cave hyena. Wolves, wild horses, and bison roamed on the bare plains exposed by the melting glaciers.

To hunt and then to butcher these animals, Paleolithic man had developed a wide range of tools. First had come the clumsy but versatile hand axe, which could do a great many things—cut, kill, stun, pierce, and serve as a missile—but which did not do any of them very well. The Clactonians of the third Ice Age had added the flake tools, sharp scrapers that could be used for cutting up carcasses and dressing skins. The Mousterian-Neanderthal culture that followed had contributed knives, awls, and weapon points, as well as the technique of retouching to afford a sharper edge.

With the coming of the Upper Paleolithic, many new designs and new materials were invented. Louis de Mortillet called this fertile period of invention the

Aurignacian Period, with the Cro-Magnon people as its main representative. Until the 1930's, that view was generally accepted. Then it became apparent that the label was not exact enough. The Aurignacian had to be divided into several subperiods in order to account for local variations in toolmaking technique.

Just where these divisions should be made is still a topic of heated scientific debate. It is easy to give names to large periods of cultural development, but there is always fierce fighting among the specialist scholars about the fine details. It will do, however, to follow this system of dividing the Aurignacian:

The *Chatelperronian* phase is the earliest. It is named for a site at Chatelperron in western France, and its typical product is a large, curved flint knife with one edge razor-sharp and the other blunt. This style of fashioning flints originated in southeast Asia, and probably the Chatelperronian people entered Europe after dwelling in the Orient.

Next came a wave of immigrants whose culture we call the *Aurignacian proper*. Their advance into Europe can be traced by the trail of distinctive artifacts they left behind: from eastern Asia to the Crimea to the Balkans to central Europe to France. By the time they got to France, they found the Chatelperronians already established there. Doubtless there was some friction between the two cultural groups, but they seem to have tolerated one another and lived side by side.

These people were the Cro-Magnons. Their flint tools were finer than any previous ones, with a wide range of types of knives and scrapers. They developed a method of striking long bladelike flakes from cores of flint, and this in turn allowed the introduction of new and highly useful tools like the chisel. Once in possession of chisels, the Cro-Magnons were able to begin fashioning tools from a material impossible to use easily before: bone.

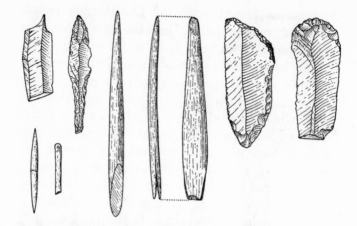

*Aurignacian implements and carvings.*

They made polished bone pins and awls, and spear-heads that could be fastened to wooden shafts. Given the necessary tools, bone is far easier to work than stone; so once they had their chisels, the Cro-Magnon Aurignacians could turn out a wealth of new implements that led to still further advances. In this way, one key invention touches off a cascade of progress, and the rate of advance is forever increasing.

The third Aurignacian phase is known as the *Gravettian*—named not for a place but for a type of tool, the *gravette,* a sharp cutting and engraving device shaped something like the blade of a penknife. The Gravettians were a widespread people who roamed eastern and central Europe and reached as far west as Spain, France, and England. They hunted the big game that flourished at the borders of the northern ice sheet, and used their gravettes to decorate the ivory bangles they made from the tusks of mammoths. These people also were fond of carving small female statuettes that we call "Venuses"—

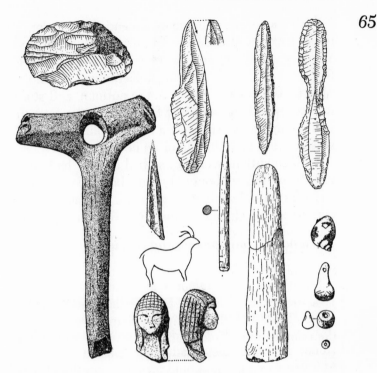

plump little creatures that probably had a religious significance.

Chatelperronians, Aurignacians, Gravettians—these people of twenty-five to thirty thousand years ago were distinct cultural groups, yet they clearly shared a common outlook on the world and can all be classed under the general heading of Aurignacians. They inhabited an unkind world bleak with snow. A sheet of mile-thick ice covered northern Europe, reaching as far south as what is now England, Germany, and Poland. South of this uninhabitable ice field, conditions were not much more cheerful. There were few great forest trees. Scrubby birches and alders sprouted from the frozen earth.

**66**

From every mountain there descended a glacier, a river of ice, to spread over the surrounding territory. Winters were long and harsh, with heavy snowfalls that probably made hunting difficult or impossible. Men had to kill their meat in the autumn, and store it during the long winter of huddling in the cave. It was a dangerous existence; a sudden blizzard out of season could take the life of an entire tribe.

Still, conditions were not so bad as they had been twenty or thirty thousand years before, when the Neanderthals alone battled the cold. And now a man could see the climate changing within his lifetime, the weather a little warmer than it had been in his grandfather's day, and warmer yet in the manhood of his grandchildren.

Since hunting mammoths and rhinoceroses is no task for a man alone, we believe that the Aurignacians moved in tribal groups, perhaps large families dominated by one old man or woman. Within each group the various members had special functions. The strong young men, of course, were the hunters of big game. The women, probably, tended the fires of the home hearth, made clothing from hides, and gathered seeds and nuts to add to the diet of meat. Children may have helped by catching fish and hunting rabbits and birds. There was a group of craftsmen within each tribe, too, those who contrived the stone knives and spear points, the awls and needles of bone, the hatchets and chisels and gouges. Old men too slow to hunt any more, young men crippled by accidents or maimed at birth—these must have been the makers of tools.

And then there were the artists.

The supreme contribution of the Aurignacians to mankind may have been art. If there was any Neanderthal art, we do not know of it. A crude clay statue of a bear, found in a French cave, possibly is Neanderthal work, but there is no proof of that. Not

until the arrival of the Aurignacians do works of art
become part of the archaeological picture.

When a tribe must devote all its energy to the basic task of finding enough food to stay alive, there is no time for such luxuries as art. No one can be spared to draw pictures or carve ornaments. Yet it seems that even the earliest men may have had a love of beauty, which is the seed of art. The ape-men of China, half a million years ago, brought glittering crystals of quartz to their caves near Peking. Perhaps they collected them for their lovely sparkle. Some of the Acheulian hand axes, too, are more lovingly fashioned than mere choppers need to be, and possibly their makers took an artistic pride in the patterns they formed as they chipped their flints into shape.

It is a long way, though, from quartz crystals and attractive hand axes to full-scale works of art. The Neanderthals, hard pressed by the grimness of their Ice Age environment, may not have had time for art; but the Aurignacians, living in a warmer climate and equipped with new tools that made existence easier, burst forth with a flourish of artistic endeavor that is one of the glories of human achievement.

Édouard Lartet was the discoverer of Aurignacian art. During his investigations of the caves and rock shelters of the Dordogne in the 1860's, Lartet found many tools of bone and horn on which pictures of animals had been scratched or carved. Some were knives with reindeer-shaped handles; some were spear-throwing devices in the form of horses' heads or crouching lions; some were long engraved scepters of no readily understood function. Then, too, Lartet found rough plaques of bone or stone on which the images of animals were drawn: mammoths, horses, reindeer, bison. The pictures were done skillfully, and there was no doubt of what they were intended to represent.

It was startling to contemplate these little

*Stone Age engravings.*

sketches. They were not masterpieces by any standards, but the fact that they existed at all was impressive. They showed that Aurignacian man, however occupied in the struggle for food, had taken time to scrawl quick pictures of the animals that he hunted, and even a few awkward human figures. Somehow that knowledge made him seem more like ourselves and less a creature of mindless savagery.

Still, one could look at these bits of engraved bone with a kind of tolerant amusement. How quaint! How primitive! How charming! That was the attitude that prevailed in 1880 when Don Marcelino de Sautuola made public the existence of the amazing art gallery in the cave of Altamira.

Since the Altamira paintings were too good to be true, Don Marcelino was accused of faking them, and died a bitter man. Only long after his death were they recognized as genuine. Of course, they are not Aurignacian paintings; it is known that they were the work of the considerably later Magdalenian culture.

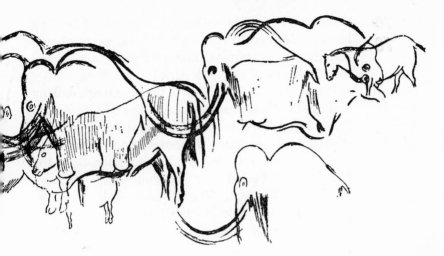

But they helped to revise our opinions of the artistic abilities of prehistoric man.

The archaeologist most closely associated with the study of the cave paintings is Henri Breuil, who died in 1961 at the age of 84. Breuil was a priest with an interest in antiquity, and he began his explorations of the caves in France in 1901. Accompanied by two other young men, he entered a cave called Les Combarelles, and found Aurignacian relics near the entrance. After crawling for two hundred yards through a passageway a few feet high, the three explorers discovered engraved figures of reindeer, mammoths, bears, lions, and even a dancing man on the walls.

At the cave of Font de Gaume, half a mile away, an even more startling array of paintings awaited them: eighty portraits of bison, forty horses, twenty-three mammoths, seventeen reindeer, eight wild cattle, four antelopes, two woolly rhinoceroses, a bear, a wolf, and a lioness! Breuil's future career was

70

determined on that exciting day. The rest of his long life was devoted to the discovery and study of prehistoric cave paintings, first in France and Spain, then as far afield as South Africa.

Breuil classified and dated the paintings, linking them to the tools found in association with them. He learned that the cave paintings were without exception Upper Paleolithic. There were none earlier than the Aurignacian Period, and none later than the Magdalenian Period that had ended this phase of man's development. The Neanderthals had not painted pictures, nor did the farming peoples who emerged after the close of the fourth and final Ice Age.

Breuil showed that there were several phases of cave art, marking stages in man's mastery of artistic skill. The early Aurignacians drew simple outline figures in yellow, black, or red, sometimes filling them in with masses of a single color. The animals were drawn in profile, seemingly motionless, with

*Impressionistic reindeer engravings.*

only two legs represented, one in front and one in back. The puzzle of how to depict antlers, horns, or tusks was a tough one, and the early artists solved it by twisting the heads of their animals around so that they were seen full face while the rest of the creature was done in profile.

Gradually, shading and perspective were mastered. The artists learned how to use three or four tones of color in the same drawing, and how to render all four limbs in a realistic way. They discovered the secrets of representing motion. They found ways of imitating three-dimensional solidity. They employed an almost photographic technique to show muscles and texture of hide.

Then, in the final phase, this extreme realism gave way to a kind of abstract art. As though bored with their accomplishments, the artists no longer bothered to fill in every detail. They invented clever ways of showing a great deal with a few strokes. To represent a herd of reindeer they would paint only the first and

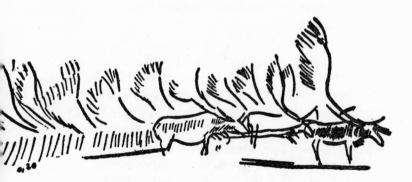

72

*Abstract*

last animals in detail, with a forest of antlers and legs between them to stand for the others. A few quick lines gave the basic shape of a mammoth; sometimes the paintings were so abstract that they were nothing but geometrical patterns. It is the kind of stripped-down, austere art that only great masters can employ. The artist cuts through the surface appearance to show the underlying essentials.

*Materials*

The paints used by the cave artists were made from powdered minerals mixed with clay and animal blood. Ocher, or iron oxide, provided pigments of red, orange, yellow, and chocolate brown, depending on the impurities present. Oxides of manganese gave brown and blue-black. The deepest blacks were obtained by grinding burned bone. Mortars and pestles used for grinding these pigments have been discovered, along with holders for storing them once they had been prepared. The holders were made from shells, hollow stones, shafts of bone fitted with stoppers, and even human skulls. Palettes of bone served for the mixing of colors.

*Painting the picture*

The actual painting of the pictures must have been an extraordinarily difficult affair. The caves were dark, so the artists had to work by the flickering light of torches or the faint glow of wicks set in animal fat. In many caves the artists deliberately chose the most inaccessible places for their works: as far from the entrance as possible, and so high on the walls that they must have had to paint standing on the shoulders of assistants. Toiling in cold, clammy caves, twisting their bodies into uncomfortable positions, they patiently applied their pigments to the damp walls. First they sketched an outline with charcoal, or scratched it in with a stone, and then, usually working with their fingers, they applied their paints.

Fingers alone could not have achieved the full range of effects found in Upper Paleolithic art. Quite likely the artists made brushes for themselves by chewing the ends of twigs, though of course none of these have been preserved. It also appears that some of their shading effects were obtained by using pads of moss or fur to spread the paint. The most delicate effects of all were achieved through a kind of spatter-painting, and the artists may have taken paint into their mouths and sprayed it through tubes against the walls.

For a long time the Aurignacians were regarded only as the crude forerunners of the great artists of Magdalenian times. The finest paintings all came from such Magdalenian caves as Altamira, and the known Aurignacian works seemed like the hesitating attempts of uncertain pioneers. That opinion had to be scrapped in September 1940 when the cave of Lascaux was discovered by four teenage boys.

The leader of the group was eighteen-year-old Marcel Ravidat. Accompanied by sixteen-year-old Georges Agnel and two fifteen-year-old friends, Ravidat entered a hole in the ground that had been revealed many years before by the uprooting of a tree. Some townsfolk of the little French village claimed that the hole, a yard wide and a yard deep, led to a secret underground passage built during the Middle Ages.

Carrying a lamp, Ravidat crawled down into the hole and found that it opened into another, much narrower shaft. Pebbles dropped into that shaft took a long time to strike bottom. The boys widened the opening, and Ravidat slithered through, head first. His friends followed him. They were in an underground cavern. Moving slowly, for the lamp gave only a dim light, they reached a narrow, high-roofed chamber and saw traces of colored paintings on the wall.

They were well aware of the many prehistoric grottoes of art that had been found in France, and suspected that they had discovered another. "Our joy was beyond description," Marcel Ravidat wrote a few days later. "A bunch of wild Indians doing a war-dance wouldn't have equalled us." Keeping silent about their discovery for the time being, they returned the next day with more powerful flashlights, and were awed to realize that they had come upon not merely another prehistoric art gallery, but the finest one in all of France.

Four gigantic black bulls, three times larger than life, capered across the ceiling. A leaping cow arched over a group of little horses. Two shaggy bison, back to back, seemed to be racing off furiously in opposite directions. Another bison, drawn in outline, was ripped open by a spear, and beside him lay a fallen hunter. The power and the beauty of the Lascaux paintings were overwhelming. (*Photograph, page ii.*)

The boys took Leon Laval, a local schoolteacher, into their confidence. He was less than eager to climb down into the chilly cavern, but once he had seen the wonders it contained he knew what must be done: Henri Breuil had to be notified. By the following week, the famed expert on prehistoric art was at work in Lascaux. Breuil was astonished to find that these fantastic paintings belonged, not to the Magdalenian, but to the Aurignacian—which meant that at least one group of Cro-Magnon men had developed an advanced artistic technique thousands of years before the paintings of Altamira were created. The art of Lascaux is somewhat different in style from that of Altamira, but it would be wrong to say that Altamira art is an "improvement" on that of Lascaux. It simply employs different techniques— but it is not possible to improve on perfection.

We realize now that the Aurignacians could afford the luxury of a guild of artists, who must have handed their secrets down from father to son over hundreds of years. Such men may have spent all their time practicing their art, while being supported by other members of their tribe. They were the first professional artists in the world.

Having said that, we are faced with the need to explain the purpose of cave art. It is not good enough to say that the paintings were done for the sheer love of beauty. If that were so, the artists would not have taken such pains to hide their works in places where it was so difficult to see them.

Certainly the joy of craftsmanship must have been a factor in any Aurignacian artist's work, but it is felt that the paintings served a magical, rather than ornamental, purpose. The Aurignacians were a hunting society, depending on their luck as huntsmen for their lives. It is a common primitive idea that one can gain power over an animal or a man by making an image of it. The paintings in the caves, perhaps, were intended to capture the souls of the mammoths and bison and cattle and make the animals vulnerable to the shafts of the hunters. Many of the animals on the cave walls are shown with their hearts clearly outlined in red, or with bright arrow-shaped lines tracing a path to the vital organs. Surely these must be intended as magical charms to bring luck in the hunt. A number of the animals are portrayed as pregnant; can we see this as a wish that the game herds would be fruitful and multiply? We can merely guess at the ceremonies that took place in the chilly chambers within the earth—the dances, the prayers, the torchlight processions beneath the colorful images of the hunted beasts.

The footprints of the dancers can still be traced in the clay floors of some caves. The images of wizards and sorcerers, garbed in fantastic costumes, are found among the painted animals. Unknown rites were celebrated, strange magical rituals performed. The artists, then, were not mere entertainers and decorators. The life of the tribe was believed to depend on their work. (*Photograph, page iv.*)

# 5
# VENUSES
# AND
# LAUREL
# LEAVES

The cave paintings of Cro-Magnon man are the most spectacular achievements of the Aurignacian Period, and rightfully draw most of the attention. They delight the eye and dazzle the imagination. We can feel little but admiration for these long-legged pioneers who entered a Europe still locked in the grip of endless winter, made themselves its masters, staked out their hunting ranges, and left for posterity the miraculous paintings of Lascaux. But the Cro-Magnons were not the only Aurignacian people, and the others merit our praise as well.

The earliest phase of the Aurignacian, the one called the Chatelperronian, is still largely a mystery to us. The second phase, the Aurignacian proper, is the time of the Cro-Magnon people we have just been discussing. While the Cro-Magnons were glorifying the walls of the French caves, the third Aurignacian people—the Gravettians—were leading a different sort of existence to the east.

Russia, perhaps, was the place of origin for the Gravettians. They moved slowly westward across Europe until ultimately they stood at the Atlantic shores, but the core of their territory lay in the region now controlled by the Communist nations. Their hunting range was a narrow grassy strip, bordered on the south by the glaciers of the Alps and the Carpathian Mountains, and on the north by the great arctic ice sheet. In the world of twenty-five thousand years ago, the corridor between those two zones of ice was the grazing ground of vast herds of cold-weather animals: bison, reindeer, cattle, horses, and especially woolly mammoths. Wolves, leopards, and lions preyed on these animals—and so did man.

Even in an ice age, there are some seasons of relative warmth. When what passed for spring arrived, grass and small shrubs began to grow in the corridor of pastureland. The herds of grazing beasts made their way from one valley to another in a regular seasonal pattern of migration, eating their way northward in summer, returning to the southern limits of their range in winter. The Gravettians learned to lie in wait along these seasonal migration routes. They pitched their camps in valleys where they would be sheltered against blizzards, and used the side ravines running out of the valleys as natural corrals to trap the big animals. With wild shouts and flaming torches they stampeded the mammoths into dead-end gullies and slew them by hurling boulders down from above; or, where they could, they drove the mammoths over cliffs and feasted in leisure on the broken carcasses. Life was hard, but there was a steady rhythm to it, back and forth over the pasture lands in pursuit of the herds. When winter came, and a supply of meat to last until spring was safely cached, there was time to gather by firesides to chant songs of triumph, time to carve little baubles from the tusks of the slain mammoths, time to reflect on the meaning and purpose of life itself.

A good deal is known about these Gravettian mammoth-hunters, and the more we learn about them the more we realize how advanced their culture was. They painted no cave paintings, for they had no caves, but their artistic impulses found other forms of expression, and they were responsible for several important advances in human achievement. As far as we know, the Gravettians were the first human beings who built houses for themselves.

Living on the open plains, even in winter, they had to construct some sort of shelter, or perish. Archae-ologists working in Czechoslovakia, southern Russia, and Siberia have excavated a number of Gravettian houses, the oldest known man-made structures. They were large pit-houses, sunk in the ground and floored with powdered limestone. Heavy boulders were piled up to form walls. No roofs have survived, or even postholes where roof supports might have stood, and so it appears that the Gravettian houses were covered by skins weighted down by mammoth bones.

A different type of dwelling, also Gravettian, was found at Vestonice in Czechoslovakia. This was a circular hut, partly sunk into a hillside so that when covered it would have the form of an artificial cave. The remnants of wooden roof supports were found, and the roof itself probably was made of branches, grass, and earth, covered with skins and weighted with mammoth bones. A circular wall of limestone and clay bordered the little hut—the oldest wall yet discovered. Within the hut were a hearth and the fragments of an oven or kiln, in which some broken clay statuettes were found. The excavators have sug-gested that "this was no ordinary dwelling house, but

80  perhaps the quarters of a Paleolithic medicine man, the sacred den where he shaped and hardened the images of beasts and of women to be used in his hunting and fertility rites."

Another of these Gravettian huts from Czechoslovakia reveals that these mammoth-hunters understood the use of coal for fuel. Logs were scarce on the practically treeless plains, and outcroppings of coal lay quite close to the surface; but the discovery that the black mineral could be used for fires must have been the work of a keen observer with a roving, inquisitive mind.

House-builders, coal-users—already the Gravettians seem more complex than we usually imagine prehistoric man of this era to have been. And the evidence from the best-known Gravettian site, the Czechoslovakian town of Predmost, makes these mammoth-hunters stand out even more sharply in our imaginations.

The region of Czechoslovakia known as Moravia is an extremely fertile agricultural area. The soil is the soft, fine, yellowish material known as *loess,* which yields productive crops. In the middle of the nineteenth century a Moravian farmer named Josef Crometschek reaped a harvest of an unusual sort while ploughing his fields near Predmost: a vast deposit of the bones of animals and human beings, stone tools, and ornaments.

To Crometschek these discoveries had but one use. Bone, when ground to powder, makes excellent fertilizer. He had his workmen grind the heap of bones and spread the powder on his land. But there was such a great supply that Crometschek began selling wagonloads of bones to other farmers. He went on mining this storehouse of the past for nearly thirty years before Czech archaeologists learned in 1878 of what was going on.

Soon the archaeologists persuaded Crometschek

to sell his land to a museum, and by 1884 the excavators were at work. Six to ten feet below the surface was a layer of ancient deposits nearly a yard thick, a dark stripe easily detected against the yellow background of the loess. It contained the ashes of innumerable fires and the bones of the great beasts of the Ice Age, chiefly those of the woolly mammoth.

The archaeologists soon realized that they were at work on an Aurignacian hunting camp that had been occupied for hundreds of years. The bones of more than a thousand individual mammoths were found, even after decades of casual destruction of the deposits for use as fertilizer. That showed how capable a hunter Aurignacian man had been. The image of him as a timid, helpless creature barely able to cope with the hardships of life, which some prehistorians had suggested, was shattered. Here on the open wind-raked plains, these early hunters had sought out and destroyed by the hundreds the seemingly invincible woolly mammoths. No mere wanderers, they had pitched a permanent camp at Predmost, occupying a key position along the migration routes of the big animals. Lying in wait for the ponderous herds, the Predmost people had come forward to trap their prey, and then to feast.

Karl Maska, one of the Czech archaeologists who worked at Predmost, reported a major discovery in the enormous bone field in the summer of 1894. Working at a depth of nine feet in the loess, he uncovered a layer of stones thirteen feet long, nine feet wide, and sixteen inches thick. Below it was a mass grave whose walls were formed from the shoulder blades and skulls of mammoths. Within lay the skeletons of nearly fifty people, close together in a squatting position. No other objects were found with them, except for a necklace of forty oval beads of ivory around the neck of a child.

The reasons for this mass burial must always re-

82 main time's mystery. An epidemic, a sudden blizzard, a famine, even a deliberate human sacrifice—we do not know. But the mere existence of the grave tells us much about these people. They took great care to protect the bodies, surrounding them with the massive bones of the beasts that yielded food, and covering the grave with a blanket of stones to ward off foxes or hyenas. Reverence for the dead indicates a belief in the existence of a soul, a spirit that survives the mere body. A whole constellation of religious and philosophical attitudes can be inferred from a single grave. Generally, prehistoric man was content to toss his dead on a rubbish heap, or leave them exposed in the open air. That is why we have so few skeletons of Lower Paleolithic man. These hunters of Upper Paleolithic times had a different outlook toward the dead, and archaeologists, eager for a glimpse of early man, are grateful to them for it.

The Predmost excavations also brought to light thousands of flint tools: knives, choppers, chisels, and other implements in the Gravettian style that were needed to cut up the mammoth meat. Curiously, no heavy weapons have ever been found, so that we must guess how the Gravettians slew their prey.

With excellent stone tools at their command and an unlimited supply of ivory, it is not surprising that the Gravettians produced many carved ornaments of that material. Small disks of ivory, polished cylinders and cones, oval plaques, and other such objects have been found at many Gravettian sites. The most famous works of Gravettian art, however, are the little female statues known as "Venuses."

These were generally carved from mammoth tusks, but the best known of all was made of limestone. This is the Venus of Willendorf, discovered in Austria in 1908. A laborer mending a road spied it first. It is about four inches high, and portrays a fat woman with enormous bosom and thighs, tiny arms, and a strangely featureless face completely hidden by what perhaps is a braided hair-do. The workman took the little figure into the town of Willendorf, where a traveling archaeologist named Szombathy had taken up lodgings. Herr Szombathy was delighted by the grotesque figurine, which he named the Venus of Willendorf even though this "Venus" was hardly beautiful by the standards of modern times.

Since then, many other Venuses have been found in Gravettian deposits. Some of them are so crude that it is barely possible to see what they are. All have exaggerated female characteristics, though the figures often are eerie and abstract, like the Venus of Lespugue, found in France in 1922. This ivory statuette, six inches high, shows a strange-looking woman whose body is vastly enlarged at the hips and thighs, but tapers away to weird slimness at top and bottom. (*Photograph, page v.*)

The Gravettian Venuses clearly were not intended as portraits of actual women. Their oddly distorted proportions lead us to think that they were ritual objects used in some cult of fertility. They exaggerate the areas of the female form that have to do with childbirth, and dismiss the rest as irrelevant. We have already noted that the paintings of pregnant animals in the French and Spanish caves were a possible fertility device. To the Aurignacian hunters, childbirth must have been the miracle of miracles, bringing new life to the sparse tribes. A tiny pot-bellied carving of the Gravettian Venus, perhaps, was a fertility charm that was thought to bring the bounty of birth.

Aurignacian man entered Europe about thirty thousand years ago, at a time when the weather was gradually warming. During this period of milder climate he was able to spread over much of the continent and to develop his distinctive forms of art. The change in the weather, though, was not permanent. After some five thousand years the trend reversed itself and the glaciers crept southward again.

In this time of new cold, a change came over the people of western Europe. The Aurignacian culture disappeared, and a culture called the Solutrean emerged. Sharply different from the cultures that had gone before and those that followed after, the Solutreans have been a riddle to archaeologists.

Édouard Lartet and Henry Christy were the first to find Solutrean artifacts. During their work in the Dordogne in 1863, they found at the rock shelter of Laugerie Haute three levels of occupation marked by changes in the style of making flint blades. The lowest and the middle level were two phases of the Aurignacian, but the flints of the topmost level were

*Solutrean implements and carvings.*

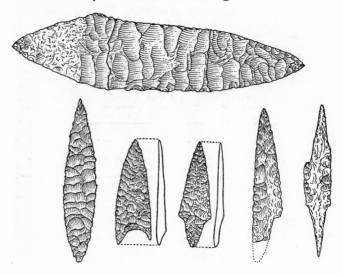

strikingly different: long and tapering and remarkably thin, with elegant retouching on both sides. Because these handsome blades were much longer than they were broad, they quickly became known as "laurel-leaf points" and "willow-leaf points."

Lartet and Christy referred to this style as "the industry of Laugerie Haute." But that was an awkward name, and risked confusion with finds made at nearby Laugerie Basse. Therefore, when laurel-leaf and willow-leaf blades were discovered a few years later at the site of Solutré in eastern France, the name Solutrean was coined for this culture.

Later archaeologists found Solutrean artifacts above the Aurignacian at many sites in western Europe. Everything about them indicated that some entirely new group of people had taken possession of Spain and France. The Solutrean flints were utterly unlike Aurignacian ones; these flat, amazingly

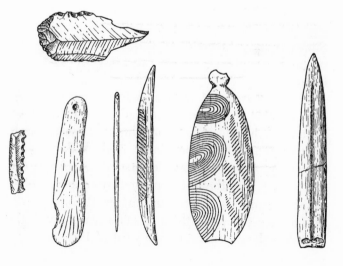

attractive blades displayed almost incredible craftsmanship. It was craftsmanship enjoyed for its own
sake, too, for many of the Solutrean stone implements
could have had no practical use. Some were too thin
and fragile; some were of bizarre shapes; some were
made from brightly colored stone such as chalcedony
and jasper, and were obviously intended only as
ornaments. The few Solutrean wall paintings and
sculptures that have been found are also novel in
style.

For a while archaeologists spoke of a Solutrean
"empire"—a conquered zone dominated by aggressive invaders. They tried to trace the path of conquest by searching for Solutrean-style blades in other
areas. Some argued that the Solutreans had come
from North Africa; others said from Hungary, since
in both places flints with some resemblance to the
Solutrean ones were found. Prehistorians developed
a picture of a triumphant army sweeping westward
or northward into the Aurignacian territory: a fully
developed culture from elsewhere suddenly arriving
to overthrow the Cro-Magnon men and impose their
own way of life.

This view has been challenged in recent years. In
April, 1959, a Canadian archaeologist, Philip E. L.
Smith of the University of Toronto, returned to the
original Lartet-Christy site at Laugerie Haute to
begin a study of the entire Solutrean mystery.

The rich trove of archaeological treasure in the
rock shelters of the Dordogne had by no means been
exhausted in the nearly one hundred years since
Lartet's work. Laugerie Haute itself had been re-
visited by French archaeologists in the 1920's, but
more than half the site remained untouched when
Smith began his work. The Upper Paleolithic deposits were ten yards thick in some places, with the
Solutrean levels covering one yard of this.

Smith carefully cleared level after level of these deposits, working downward from the most recent artifacts to the earliest. The lowest levels, he knew, were Aurignacian. Above them was a layer of limestone fragments from a partial collapse of the overhanging cliff. Above this, Smith found the earliest Solutrean relics.

They dated, he estimated, from about twenty-two thousand years ago, a time of extreme cold when Laugerie Haute and perhaps most of the Dordogne had been abandoned by the Aurignacians. A band of Solutrean people had arrived at the rock shelter and briefly made camp there. They left behind some of their blades—not the marvelous slender ones of their later period, but nevertheless blades that already were distinctly Solutrean in style, carefully retouched and elegantly tapered.

Some time later, the Solutreans returned to Laugerie Haute, and now they remained in residence for several thousand years. Carbon-14 dating showed an age of about twenty thousand years for this new settlement. Close study enabled Smith to identify many successive stages of improvement in their blades. The points, he wrote, "become finer and more carefully retouched until, in the final early Solutrean level, the more archaic types disappear and the retouching invades much of the opposite face of the blade." In more recent levels, the true laurel-leaf points appear. According to Smith, "the Solutrean craftsmen show an amazing flair for experimenting with the forms of the laurel leaves. Some are tiny and delicate; others are long and thick. Many are long and slender, and the retouching consists of fine parallel flaking. Some have such thin cross sections that it is difficult to imagine how they could have served any utilitarian purpose. Indeed, they may have been showpieces and luxury items."

88     A still later development was the willow-leaf point, with rounded ends and extremely delicate retouching. It replaced the larger and more tapered laurel-leaf point in popularity midway in the Solutrean. Another Solutrean contribution was the true needle with an eye for threading. Solutrean needles, made of bone, are the oldest that have been discovered. The eyes were quite small, and Philip Smith believes that such needles "were used for fine stitching or to produce fitted clothing."

About seventeen thousand years ago the trend toward colder weather once more halted, and the climate of western Europe became unusually mild. This was apparently no boon to the Solutreans, who had endured the long cold spell with ease. The big game such as the woolly mammoth, uncomfortable in a warm climate, moved northward out of France. As their sources of food grew scarcer, the Solutreans dwindled in numbers. The shelter at Laugerie Haute was abandoned. Other Solutrean outposts soon were deserted also. After some four thousand years, the Solutreans disappeared as mysteriously as they had come, and a new culture, the Magdalenian, flourished in western Europe.

The Magdalenians were much closer in their ways to the long-vanished Aurignacians than they were to the Solutreans. The cave paintings of the Magdalenians, their flint and bone tools, and their other artifacts all show descent from Aurignacian models. So the Solutreans were intruders who did not fit into the general pattern of Upper Paleolithic life in that part of the world. They came, they thrived, and they vanished, and when they were gone they left no heirs. The Aurignacian peoples must have continued to hold the regions bordering on the Solutrean dominion, and after the Solutreans had departed, the older culture-group returned, transformed now into the Magdalenian.

The political pattern of Europe of seventeen thousand years ago is likely to remain a matter of guesswork forever. The alliances, the shifts of allegiance, the migrations of tribes, the local wars—all these things can only be dimly perceived, if at all, from the flint deposits in the caves. One thing does seem clear now, thanks to Philip Smith's work. The Solutrean culture did not develop in some other part of the world and arrive fully matured in western Europe. The earliest stages of the Solutrean have been detected in the caves of France. In the midst of the Aurignacian folk, a new and unusual culture evolved, carried its distinctive traits through what formerly had been the territory of the Aurignacian Cro-Magnons, and disappeared after a reign of four thousand years.

We who see time in small units regard four thousand years as an incredibly long span. It is, of course; and it seemed just as long to the Solutreans. The Solutrean people of eighteen thousand years ago could look back on a line of generations stretching into the infinite past. It must have seemed to them that they had always inhabited the valleys of southern France, and that they always would.

Yet against the larger span of Paleolithic times the Solutrean episode lasted but a moment. When we think of the Abbevilleans chipping hand axes in an unvarying way for a hundred thousand years or more, we see how brief the Solutreans' time really was. But the pace of progress was accelerating, now. Man was becoming a quick learner. Great revolutions lay just beyond the horizon, and now one culture would succeed another with ever-increasing rapidity.

# 6
# THE END
# OF THE OLD
# STONE AGE

The Magdalenians who occupied Europe about seventeen thousand years ago lived at the end of an era. Certainly they did not realize that, for they had no way of sensing the patterns of human events, the ebb and flow of cultures, the overriding picture of the hundred and fifty centuries of the Upper Paleolithic. They had no written history, and so they could not carry their awareness back more than a few generations. The tongues of old men might describe how it was in bygone days, but not with any depth of understanding.

We have reconstructed the archives of the past that prehistoric men neglected to provide. We have learned how to read the records in the earth: the fossil record and the geological record and the record of the stone tools. We see the pattern that the Magdalenians could not have perceived.

92     What we see is European man's million-year
struggle with the glaciers. Four great Ice Ages had
shaped the pattern of events in Europe, turning man
into the toy of the elements. Whole populations had
been driven into refuge, had returned thousands of
years later, had been driven out again. Slowly man
learned to cope with the forces that bedeviled him;
he brought fire under control, wrapped himself in
animal hides, and endured the cold rather than flee-
ing from it. The Aurignacian Period marked man's
forward progress clearly. Now he could consider
himself practically immune to the challenge of the
ice. He was able to hold his own in frozen Europe.

Of course, short-term shifts in the weather outlook
could affect his existence. A few decades of relatively
warm weather would drive the woolly beasts to new
pastures, and force man to follow. A return to the
cold meant a sudden revival of the habits and tactics
of Ice Age life. Tribes had to be able to adapt to
these changes.

What the Magdalenian people could not know is
that the glaciers now were permanently on the wane.
The fourth Ice Age at last was over, after several
false thaws. From now on, each year would be infini-
tesimally warmer than the one before, so that over
the centuries and the tens of centuries an entirely
new climate would appear. There would be sweeping changes in the kinds of animal and plant life as
well. Upper Paleolithic man would have exciting new
opportunities, and his old way of life would of necessity be abandoned.

The Magdalenians, like the Solutreans and the
Aurignacians before them, were skilled hunters,
adapted to a bitterly cold environment and living in
caves, rock shelters, and open-air camps. Fifteen
thousand years had passed since the Aurignacian
vanguards entered Europe. The Magdalenians were

heirs to all the skills that had been acquired in those fifteen thousand years. They did not suspect that shortly their skills would be of little value in a changed world.

So they were at once the highest representatives of their era, and the last. Their culture spread over a wide area. The homeland was in southwest France and northern Spain, but Magdalenian influence was felt in Belgium, Switzerland, southern Germany, and Czechoslovakia. The Magdalenian way of life owed much to the Gravettian mammoth-hunters of eastern Europe, though it was more directly descended from the Cro-Magnon people of the Aurignacian proper.

The Aurignacians had introduced many new tools of stone and bone. They were responsible for the long bladelike flint knife with parallel sides, and for the beak-pointed chisel or burin. From bone they manufactured awls, pins, dart points, tubes to hold paint, and beads and other body ornaments.

The Magdalenians preserved this heritage and extended it. They took nothing from the Solutreans except that useful gadget, the sewing needle. Magdalenian stone tools do not resemble the elegant Solutrean flints at all. Instead they returned to the Aurignacian traditions. A favorite Magdalenian tool was the long straight-sided knife, made by detaching a series of regular flakes from blocks of flint. This was accomplished by placing a punch of bone in the proper position on the flint and striking it sharply with a hammer stone. A skilled worker could rapidly slice off many flakes of the desired shape with single blows.

Where the Magdalenians really excelled was in the working of bone, horn, and ivory. They improved the simple Aurignacian bone spear point almost out of recognition, changing its base to afford a better mating of point and shaft, altering its design to make

94 it sharper and more attractive, and finally adding barbs so that a spear, once cast, could not be shaken loose by the wounded animal.

The idea of a barbed point led to the Magdalenian invention of the harpoon. Reindeer antlers were used, at first with notches cut as barbs along only one side, then on both sides. Unlike a spear point, a harpoon easily detached itself from its shaft after a blow had been struck; but a line fastened to the harpoon head allowed the hunter to keep his prey from escaping.

Another example of Magdalenian cleverness was the spear-thrower, often known by its Aztec name of *atlatl*. This device, which has been independently invented by primitive peoples in many parts of the world, seems first to have been used by the Aurignacians, but the Magdalenians gave it much wider employment. The *atlatl* is a rod about two feet long, with a prong at one end into which the butt of a spear or harpoon can be inserted. The thrower grasps the *atlatl* by the other end, cocks his arm, and hurls the weapon. Basically, the *atlatl* serves to lengthen the arm of the thrower, allowing him to impart greater force to the cast of the weapon. It requires considerable training to use properly, and its presence in the Magdalenian deposits shows that they were a people who were capable of patience and persistence.

Patience and persistence certainly were needed to produce the works of art that are the most impressive achievements of the Magdalenian Period. Cave art reached its highest point among these people. The glowing masterpieces of Altamira and other Spanish and French caves testify to the compelling power of Magdalenian painters.

Other forms of Magdalenian art are also of a high standard. Like the Gravettians, they made use of engraving tools to carve ivory and bone; but their tools were much more suited for fine work, and the results are remarkable. Spear-throwers of bone and reindeer antler were embellished with the carved images, in high relief, of the animals against which the implement was likely to be used: reindeer, mammoth, and wild horse, particularly. Batons of deeply engraved ivory, statuettes of the Gravettian Venus type, engravings of animal outlines, and small sculptured ivory horses and reindeer all display Magdalenian skill at its highest. (*Photograph, page vii.*)

It was a glittering epoch in the time of man. Food was plentiful, the climate was kind, and the dwellers in the rock shelters had the leisure necessary to stimulate progress. A rush of new techniques, new ideas, new accomplishments marked this golden age. There was a considerable increase in population also; the improvements in hunting weapons and the milder climate permitted the growth of larger tribes as food became more easily obtainable.

That very mildness of climate was eventually the undoing of the brilliant Magdalenian civilization, though. The glaciers retreated, leaving bare plains of thawing ground. Birch and willow trees sprang up, and then pines. The Ice Age animals were unable to exist in a forest environment. They were grazers, needing open grasslands, and the new birch thickets were no place for bulky beasts like the woolly mammoth. Nor did they find the warmer weather comfortable.

The herds of mammoths, reindeer, bison, and horses migrated northward, or died out altogether in the shifting climate. The Magdalenian cave dwellers found themselves deprived of the large animals that had been man's quarry since the beginning of the Ice Age. It was a time of transition, a time of doubt and trouble as an entire way of life

96    collapsed. Those Magdalenians who could not imagine any sort of existence except hunting reindeer and mammoths moved northward, following their prey toward the still-frozen steppe country of Scandinavia. The ones who remained behind developed a new pattern of culture.

Those who give names to epochs regard the Upper Paleolithic as ending with the final retreat of the glaciers. A new age began, which we call the Mesolithic, or Middle Stone Age. The Mesolithic was an era of change, a bridge linking the greatness of the Old Stone Age's final phase to the revolutionary New Stone Age that lay ahead.

The nineteenth-century archaeologists like Lartet and Mortillet had imagined that at the end of the Paleolithic the Magdalenians simply migrated northward after the big game, leaving western Europe completely empty. Now it is known that no such wholesale abandonment took place. The cultures of those who remained, though, give an impression of poverty, of shallowness, of drabness, after the grandeur of the Magdalenian.

The first of these Mesolithic cultures of western Europe was the Azilian. It gets its name from the cavern of Mas d'Azil in the French Pyrenees. Here, in 1887, a French archaeologist named Édouard Piette found nine different culture levels, one above another. He recognized five of them as Paleolithic, from Aurignacian through Magdalenian. The three most recent levels he also identified as belonging to farming folk of the New Stone Age. But the sixth level from the bottom—the one between the Magdalenian and the New Stone Age deposits—was unfamiliar.

This level contained no reindeer bones, for that arctic creature had gone north. Instead, the huntsmen of what Piette called the Azilian Period had preyed on the red deer, which had become common in the new forests of France. The tools and weapons of the Azilians were extremely small: tiny slivers of flint shaped as miniature blades or arrow points. These miniatures are known as *microliths,* or "small stones." The delicate Azilian microliths were better suited for forest hunting, evidently, than the larger stone implements developed at a time when men hunted in open prairies.

Along with the small Azilian implements, Piette found hundreds of pebbles daubed with paint. Dots, crosses, patterns of parallel lines, and random blobs were the designs on these pebbles. They are the closest that the Azilians came to art, for they neither produced statuettes nor painted scenes on cave walls. The awesome skills of the Magdalenians had perished with their civilization. The Azilians could not or perhaps would not indulge in such large-scale artistic endeavors. Pebbles daubed with colored paints satisfied their need to create things of beauty. Quite probably these mysterious pebbles had some religious significance also. (*Photograph, page vi.*)

Another Mesolithic culture had been discovered a few years earlier: the Tardenoisian, named for the French site of Tardenois. Edmond Vielle was the archaeologist who carried out the first excavations at Tardenois, in 1879. The Tardenoisians were also a forest people, whose culture took form somewhat later than that of the Azilians, and existed alongside it for a thousand years or more. The chief difference between the two is the absence of painted pebbles among the Tardenoisians. They, too, fashioned microlithic tools. Rows of tiny flint points were set in notches on shafts of bone or wood to create a complex cutting edge.

Prehistorians recognize a number of other Mesolithic cultures that existed more or less at the same

98     time. The center of new ideas seems to have been France, which was a prime cultural leader all through the Stone Age. But cultures of the Azilian and Tardenoisian type—typified by the kits of miniature stone tools—developed in much of southern and central Europe, and spread as far east as Russia. These local cultures differed in small ways from the main Azilian-Tardenoisian types, and have been given special names by the archaeologists, but these need not concern us here.

Wood was now available as it had never been in

*Mesolithic implements. Microliths, fishhook and harpoons, carvings and symbols.*

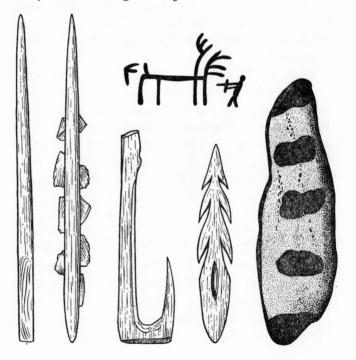

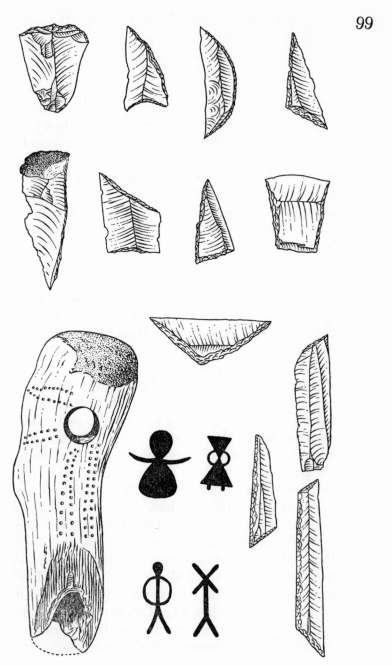

the practically treeless Ice Age world. The new
forests offered an unlimited supply of a substance
that had many possible uses. Oddly, the Mesolithic
peoples of France did not take the opportunity to
become carpenters. Their miniature tools were not
suited for chopping down trees. Instead of developing a sturdy axe, the Azilians and Tardenoisians preferred to cling to their little microlithic implements
and do without wood. Dead or fallen limbs served
them for firewood, and they probably made small
wooden objects from the branches they could break
off. But they lacked the tools that would have
allowed them to use large timber for such things as
houses, boats, or sledges.

For the first time since the arrival of the Aurignacians, then, the men of western Europe were failing
to take full advantage of their environment. They
ignored the rapidly expanding forests and lived a
reduced, impoverished life on their fringes, hunting
deer and other forest animals, trapping wild fowl
and fish, digging up edible roots.

Even less progressive were the ones who refused to
accept the change of climate at all. Instead of remaining in France and adapting even in part to the
new conditions, they went north with the Ice Age
and clung to their old ways. For these people, northern Europe, about fifteen thousand years ago, was a
new land of opportunity where they could continue
to live as their forefathers had.

During the Ice Age, a solid sheet of glaciation had
covered Scandinavia, Germany, and Poland. Now
that region was released from the clutch of permanent winter. The sheet of ice had begun to draw
back in Magdalenian times, retreating slowly but
steadily, a few yards a year. Germany was the first
region to be uncovered, and then southern Denmark
and the coasts of Norway. As the boundary of the

ice world shifted northward, the big arctic animals of Europe followed it. Some, like the woolly mammoth and woolly rhinoceros, found it impossible to adapt to the new conditions. They died out. The reindeer survived, migrating to keep close to the edges of the icecap. Northward after them came the hunters.

These were the descendants of the Magdalenian cave people, who were themselves the heirs of the Gravettian mammoth-hunters and the Cro-Magnon folk. Unwilling to take up the forest life of the microlith people and become hunters of rabbits and squirrels, these hard-bitten huntsmen were drawn ever closer to the Arctic in their struggle to preserve their way of life.

This was the only environment they found appealing: bleak and almost barren grassland, with dwarf birches and stunted willows breaking the monotony of gray-green and white, and glacier-topped mountains rising beyond the valleys and prairies. No longer able to hunt the mammoth, they tracked the reindeer herds and fell upon them with their spears and harpoons. At some point, a genius of the north devised the bow, adding a deadly new weapon to man's arsenal. So light a weapon as an arrow would have been useless against the mammoths and other huge woolly animals of the past, but now there were no more mammoths, and the new weapon was highly effective against the faster-moving but furless reindeer.

Small bands of these hunters moved through the naked landscape, killing swiftly in the short summer season before the long winter night. From June to September they slew; then they settled down to endure the cold and wait out the winter. They ate little beside venison, which they roasted over their campfires or boiled in leather vessels made of rein-

*102*   deer hide. The reindeer provided everything for their way of life: skin for their tents and clothing, antlers and bones for their tools and weapons.

The sites of the reindeer-hunters eluded archaeologists for many years. The attention of prehistorians was focused almost exclusively on France, which had been the dominant zone of European archaeology since the time of Lartet and Mortillet. The periods of prehistory were generally known by French names—Aurignacian, Magdalenian, and the rest—and in the nineteenth century there was practically no knowledge of what had taken place in the early past of other parts of Europe.

A young man named Alfred Rust brought the northern hunters to light almost singlehandedly. Rust, born in Germany in 1900, earned his livelihood as an electrician, but like many others was tempted into archaeology by casual discoveries near his own home. The countryside around his native city of Hamburg had long been a rich source of Stone Age flint blades. Every farmer, dragging his plough through the thin, sandy soil, turned up dozens of the things each spring. These flints were useless to archaeologists, because all other traces of the cultures that had produced them had long since been obliterated by ploughing. But Alfred Rust, seeing these Stone Age relics lying so close to the surface, wondered about the men who had created them. Perhaps somewhere near Hamburg a deeper layer of artifacts could be found that had never been disturbed by the local farmers.

After collecting and studying the flints for many years, Rust decided to make archaeology his profession. In 1930 he made an expedition to Syria to learn the methods of archaeology in a part of the world where the challenges were not so great as in Germany. He explored the Syrian caves, where Stone

Age settlements were easily found and readily ana-
lyzed. Only after three seasons of this valuable training did Rust turn to the archaeology of his homeland,
and now he was an expert in his field.

He learned of a meadow called Meiendorf, slightly
north of Hamburg, where unusual flints had been
found. They were not the ordinary crude blades and
heavy arrowheads that were so commonplace around
Hamburg, but flints of a kind that reminded Rust
of the ones made by the Magdalenians and the
Gravettian mammoth-hunters. One type in particular
was a distinctive scraping tool shaped at one end
like a parrot's beak. Such tools had been made in
southern Europe during the Aurignacian Period.

Rust knew that in Aurignacian times northern
Europe had been covered by ice. These unusual
flints, then, must have been the products of a later
hunting folk that came north after the shift to a
warmer climate in France. And so far nothing was
known about that northern hunting civilization.
There was a blank in northern prehistory covering
the time from fifteen thousand years ago to ten thousand years ago.

A quick inspection of Meiendorf was disappoint-
ing. Flint blades could be found in the topsoil, but
intensive farming had wiped out all other traces of
prehistoric occupation. Then Rust did some digging
in the center of the valley, and saw a layer of peat
not far below the surface. He discovered that he
was standing on top of a prehistoric lakebed. The
lake itself had vanished, but the water table was
close to the surface, and the ground was so swampy
that it had never been disturbed by farming.

Suppose, Rust reasoned, the ancient hunters had
camped by the side of this lake. They would have
thrown their debris into the water—broken tools,
discarded animal bones, and such things. There they

*104* would have remained, preserved at the bottom of the underground swamp that had replaced the lake. He began to excavate.

Carrying out an archaeological excavation in a swamp posed certain problems, naturally. Before he had dug to a depth of a yard, water was seeping into Rust's trench from all sides. He talked officials of the city of Hamburg into lending him a pump, and went on digging, down through layers of peat and mud and clay toward the original bed of the lake. In October 1933 he reached the lakebed, seven feet below the surface of the meadow. Groping in the mud, Rust pulled forth a reindeer antler four feet long. A sliver of the antler had been carefully cut away—evidently to be used in toolmaking.

He had found the camp of the reindeer-hunters. Before winter closed in, Rust had located thirty-three antlers, hundreds of reindeer bones, and forty-five flint tools of the beaked shape. The following spring, Rust returned, now as the leader of a full-scale expedition sponsored by the German Archaeological Institute. Bigger pumps were employed, and wells were bored to draw off the ground water. By the summer of 1934, the swamp was drained, and normal archaeological procedures could then be employed.

The archaeologists uncovered the remains of the ancient hunting camp: reindeer bones, antlers, flint weapons and tools, bone pins and harpoons and knives, and many other artifacts. One interesting discovery was an amber disk about two inches in diameter, covered with small sketches of animals. Each sketch had been scratched out and another drawn over it, and only the last could be seen clearly —the head and shoulders of a wild horse. Rust speculated that this was a good-luck amulet carried by the hunters as they went forth each day. Maybe the leader of the hunt scratched into the soft amber the image of the animal they hoped to catch, and scratched it out again at nightfall if they had been successful.

At the deepest point the excavators reached lay another clue to the beliefs of these hunters. They found the skeleton of a two-year-old reindeer doe, with a stone weighing twenty pounds wedged inside the ribcage. Surely this must have been a deliberate sacrifice. Perhaps the hunters weighted down the entire reindeer and hurled her into the lake as an offering to the gods, in thanks for their continued favors.

Not even the gods of the reindeer-hunters could keep the weather from growing warmer. The zone of forests crept ever northward, and the reindeer-hunters, following their herds, were pulled onward toward Sweden and Norway. In their wake came a different sort of people. They occupied the land north of the Azilian-Tardenoisian people and south of the reindeer-hunting culture. From the swamps and the forests of Denmark and Germany sprang a vigorous and inventive surge of cultural development.

# 7
# PEOPLE
# OF THE
# GREAT BOG

When man is unable to change his environment, his
environment changes him. Today, we have such
things as steam heat and air conditioning to help us
cope with the weather; we can lop down whole
forests if we do not want them; we can alter vast
areas of land by building dams and irrigation canals.
Prehistoric man, without these sweeping powers,
reacted as best he could to the changes in the world
about him, but it was always he who had to change,
not the environment.

We have seen how the end of the Ice Age, about
fifteen thousand years ago, brought grave upheavals
to early man. The great Magdalenian culture collapsed, because it was designed to function in a
climate that no longer prevailed. Some tribes lived
on the borders of the forest and hunted small game.
These were the Azilians and Tardenoisians. Others
migrated ever northward in pursuit of the cold climate they loved. These were the reindeer-hunters of

*Transition period; duration about 7,000 years.*

**AZILIAN and TARDENOISIAN CULTURES**   10,000— 8,000 B.C.   Warmer weather, heavier forests.

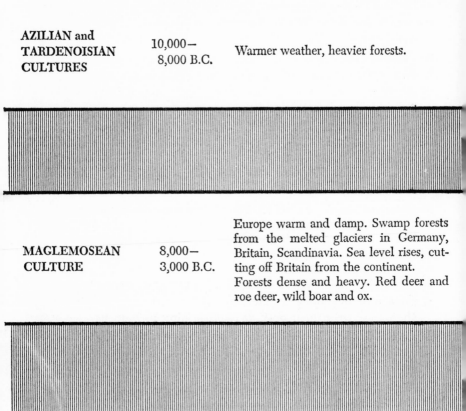

**MAGLEMOSEAN CULTURE**   8,000— 3,000 B.C.   Europe warm and damp. Swamp forests from the melted glaciers in Germany, Britain, Scandinavia. Sea level rises, cutting off Britain from the continent. Forests dense and heavy. Red deer and roe deer, wild boar and ox.

the Meiendorf meadow.

Some, who were more versatile, took advantage of the new world of the north that was opening up. As the zone of forests spread from France toward Denmark and Germany, they kept pace with the changes and turned them to their own benefit.

Prehistorians call these people the Maglemoseans, from the Danish words meaning "great bog." They lived in wet, almost swampy forests from the British

*Azilian and Tardenoisian peoples.* Transitional cultures, poorer and less artistic than Magdalenians. Microlithic tools and arrow points. Painted pebbles.

*Reindeer hunters,* remnants of Aurignacian-Magdalenian peoples, follow the game animals north, adapt to forest life. Bow and arrows, harpoons.

In the Near East, man entered the Neolithic Age by 8,000 B.C. while European man lagged behind. Agriculture, domesticated animals, pottery and settled village life developed in Asia Minor and the Fertile Crescent. Jericho was a city in 8,000 B.C.

*Maglemosean peoples,* less artistic than Magdalenians but inventive and industrious, adapt to life at shores of lakes and seas, use of wood and forest products. Microliths, stone scrapers, knives, harpoons, bows and arrows, true axes and carpentry tools.
Boats, sledges, domesticated dogs.

*Kitchen Midden people* adapt to life on the shore. Pecked and polished granite tools, first pottery.

Nea Nikomedeia, in northern Greece, dates from 6000 B.C., the oldest known Neolithic settlement in Europe. From this time on, migrants from Asia and Africa enter Europe, bringing Neolithic cultures, at first living side by side with the forest peoples, gradually replacing and driving them out as the forests are cleared for farming.

Isles to Finland, but the center of their culture was in Denmark, Germany, and southern Sweden.

Several remarkable techniques have been used to tell us not only when and where the Maglemoseans lived, but what the weather was like and even what kind of trees grew in their forests. One of these techniques, called varve-counting, was developed late in the nineteenth century by a Swedish geologist, Baron Gerhard de Geer. A varve is a ridge of gravel, sand,

*110*  and clay formed by the edge of an ice field. Baron de Geer discovered that a retreating ice field will lay down a new varve each year, marking its slight back-and-forth cycle between winter and summer. In some parts of Sweden it was possible for him to count thousands of these varves, giving a dating sequence that covered twelve thousand years. The thickness of each year's varve told him precisely what the weather was like in that year: a thin clay deposit in a cold year, a thick one in a warm year. Baron de Geer's astonishing research, which continued until his death in 1943, allowed archaeologists to pinpoint the changes in climate as accurately as though they had an almanac for Maglemosean times.

Lennart von Post, a young Swedish botanist, provided the second great technique of interpretation—pollen analysis. Post began his work upon his graduation from college in 1907, when he was twenty-three. He studied the peat deposits that had filled the lakes of Ice Age times. Peat is composed of plant debris—leaves, branches, seeds, stems—pressed down into solid form. Examining the preserved matter in a peat deposit tells what sort of plant life lived in that immediate vicinity. Post went much further than that, though, by analyzing the grains of ancient pollen that he found in the peat. Pollen is the powdery substance given off by flowers. Each type of plant or tree produces a distinctive kind of pollen, and the tiny grains are so sturdy that they last virtually forever. Lennart von Post was able to describe the forests of prehistoric Europe by identifying the pollen types that had been blown by the wind into the peat bogs of Sweden.

By combining the varve counts with the pollen record, it became possible to tell what sort of trees grew at which time, and thus to know what the weather was like. The first trees to move into northern Europe after the Ice Age were the ones that could tolerate weather that was still quite cold. These were the birch and the willow, and slightly later the pine. Around nine thousand years ago, as the weather grew still milder, the pines were dominant in the forest, but oaks, alders, and hazel were starting to appear. In another two thousand years, the temperature was too mild for pines except in northern Scandinavia, so that oak became the main forest tree. All during this time, the melting of the icecap had caused the level of the sea to rise, flooding the lowlying lands. Great Britain, which had been linked to mainland Europe, was now cut off by water. The Baltic Sea spilled over much of northern Europe, turning most of Denmark into a group of islands. As the seas moved inland, they brought along heavier rainfall, so that Europe was not only warm but damp.

This period, from ten thousand to five thousand years ago, was the time of the lively, inventive Maglemosean culture. When it began, man was a hunter and a wanderer. When it ended, he was well on his way to becoming a prosperous settled citizen.

The rediscovery of this culture began in 1900, when a team of archaeologists from the National Museum of Denmark began to dig at the Magle Mose, or "great bog," on the Danish island of Zealand. Near the surface of the site lay flint tools, but deeper in the bog were implements made from bone, antlers, and even wood. Since that time, many camps of these Maglemosean hunters have been found.

They made use of the tools of the past, such as stone scrapers and knives. They also borrowed from their Tardenoisian neighbors to the south the kit of microlithic tools, and fashioned innumerable tiny points and choppers. Where they went beyond the other Stone Age cultures was in their use of the axe.

This was not the clumsy triangular hand axe of the Lower Paleolithic, but a true axe with an attached handle. The earliest of these axes is called

*112*   the Lyngby type, after the place where it first was
discovered. It was made entirely from the antler of
the red deer, a common forest animal of the time.
The main shaft of the antler became the handle, and
a single sharpened prong was used as the cutting
edge.

This gave way to an axe blade of flint, mounted
either in an antler shaft or on a wooden handle.
Finally, the Maglemoseans developed an elaborate
axe whose flint blade was set in an antler mounting
through which a handle of wood could be inserted.

Such axes gave the Maglemoseans command of
the forest. Now they could chop trees at will and
make liberal use of the wood that was so abundant.
They became expert carpenters, inventing a broad
array of new tools. Among these were drills, gouges,
chisels, and the highly useful adze, which is an axe
with its blade mounted at right angles to the shaft
so that it can be used for scraping and hollowing logs.

The Maglemosean carpenters built boats, and
fishing now for the first time became an important
activity of man. In the past, there had always been
a little trapping of river fish, and some cultures of
the Spanish coast had depended to some extent on
what they could catch along the Atlantic shore. But
the Maglemoseans, equipped with nets, hooks, and
other fishing gear, went to sea regularly. Their boats
ranged for great distances, which explains the wide
and rapid spread of their way of life. In land, too,
they were better able to travel than any earlier culture, because they had invented the sledge. Winter
snow no longer kept men from moving about, now
that they could drag their belongings on wooden
sledges equipped with runners.

Of course, the Maglemoseans had to haul their
sledges themselves. They had no domestic draught
animals. Wild horses still roamed some parts of
Europe, but there was no way of taming and har-

nessing them at that time. Nor could the reindeer of the north yet be persuaded to serve man in this way. The Maglemoseans had just one domestic animal— the dog. And, though dogs have often been used for hauling sledges in northern lands, that development was still far in the future.

The taming of the dog was probably a matter of mutual convenience. It does not seem likely that the men of the Old Stone Age had any pets. The only dogs they knew were wolves, fierce and dangerous creatures that represented a threat to the safety of the camp. The Aurignacians must have discouraged any attempts by these wolves to approach their settlements. But, so we think, the wolves continued to lurk on the outskirts of human encampments, foraging for the scraps of meat on discarded bones. Those who were small in size and did not look so ferocious were tolerated and allowed to serve as scavengers, until at last they became part of the settlement. In return for their scraps, they took up the role of watchdogs, sounding barks of excitement whenever a stranger approached. The men also discovered that dogs were useful in hunting; a pack of tame dogs would chase a deer into exhaustion, circling it until the huntsmen could close in. Their reward would be good pickings after the kill.

As scavengers, watchdogs, and hunting companions, dogs gradually acquired a permanent role in human life. It was in Maglemosean times that this partnership of man and beast was finally established. Every Maglemosean camp shows the presence of the domestic dog.

Like all Mesolithic peoples, the Maglemoseans had little artistic ability. Nothing to compare with the cave paintings of the Upper Paleolithic came from them—nor, indeed, from any other human group until the dawn of historic times in Egypt. The Maglemoseans sometimes decorated objects of bone,

*114* antler, and amber with geometrical designs, or engraved little figures of men and animals. Along the flat rocks of the Norwegian coast they carved attractive outline designs showing reindeer, elk, whales, and seals. But mainly they were a practical folk, whose many innovations in tools and living habits were their chief claim to our admiration.

There was still nothing like a permanently occupied village. The Maglemoseans pitched their camps in one place for a few years, until their hunting parties and fishermen had thinned the food supply past the level of support, and then moved on to some other area where game and fish were more abundant. There was never any problem in finding a new campsite, since the forests were vast and the human population was small. Perhaps no more than a million people lived in all of Europe. Scattered bands of thirty or fifty individuals might wander for years without ever encountering others.

These people of the forest and lake preferred the lowlands, and rarely ventured into the high country where the more rugged reindeer-hunters roamed. Most of the lakes beside which the Maglemoseans camped have since filled up and turned into bogs, which has made things at once very interesting and very complicated for archaeologists. They must work in wet, soggy ground when excavating Maglemosean sites; but the same moisture that causes so much discomfort for them is also responsible for preserving artifacts that otherwise would have been lost. Contrary to popular belief, materials like wood and bone do not rot and decay in wet surroundings. As long as they remain uninterruptedly submerged, they can last virtually forever.

One famous Maglemosean site is Star Carr, in Yorkshire, England. Beginning in 1949 a group of Cambridge University archaeologists excavated this waterlogged settlement. At that time, practically nothing was known about the British phase of the Maglemosean. Nearly all the work on the period had been done in Scandinavia.

When the Cambridge people began to dig at Star Carr, they made an immediate and surprising discovery: the site was much older than they had expected. It had been thought that the Maglemosean way of life had taken many centuries to spread from Scandinavia to Great Britain. But the bog at Star Carr contained mostly birch trees, with a scattering of pines, and the birch forest was the first that had grown after the thawing of the ice. Carbon-14 dating showed that the Star Carr outpost had been inhabited about ten thousand years ago.

The site covered about 350 square yards. "Hardly more than three or four families can have occupied it at once," wrote the Cambridge archaeologist Grahame Clark, who led the work. "The people evidently wanted to live as near the lake as possible, for they pitched their camp directly on the reeds bordering the open water. They threw down quantities of birch brushwood, interspersed with stones and wads of clay, to help consolidate the yielding surface of the swamp. The inhabitants must have sheltered in skin tents or temporary huts."

The Maglemoseans of Star Carr were active hunters, and the remains of many animals were found. Since the deposits of bones and antlers would crack and crumble if they were allowed to dry out, the archaeologists had to place the specimens in a vacuum chamber and spray them with a plastic, polyvinyl acetate, in order to preserve them for study. "The foremost victim of the Star Carr hunters," wrote Dr. Clark, "was the red deer. Roe deer, elk, beaver, and two races of wild ox were also fairly common. In addition there were a few remains of wild pig, fox, wolf, marten, badger and single bones of a hare and hedgehog." The presence of the bones of many

*116*   kinds of birds showed that the Star Carr people had enjoyed a remarkably varied diet. Strangely, though they lived beside a lake, there were no fishbones in the camp debris. That they did fish, however, was indicated by the discovery of a piece of a wooden paddle—the oldest implement of water navigation yet found anywhere in the world.

From the swampy bog came the sort of material from which a skilled archaeologist can reconstruct an entire way of life. A group of birch stumps showed the marks of axes, and nearby lay the axes themselves. Axes that are constantly used need to be resharpened, and the only way a stone axe can be honed is by striking flakes from its cutting edge. Many of these scattered flakes were found. Other flint tools of Star Carr included scrapers and chisels. The scrapers were employed for cleansing hides to be used for clothing, tents, and perhaps boats. The chisels were needed to make spear points and harpoon heads.

Though most Maglemoseans chose to make their spear points from bone, the Star Carr people preferred the antlers of red deer. They used flint chisels to gouge out splinters of antler three to fourteen inches long, and notched a row of pointed barbs along one edge. These spearheads were fixed to long wooden shafts.

The curious little microlithic tools that were so useful to a forest people were also present at Star Carr. "Among the commonest kinds," Dr. Clark wrote, "were tiny pointed flakes, some of which were used to tip arrows and others as barbs set lower down the shaft. These small flints were held in position by resin, perhaps distilled from birch bark as in stone-age Switzerland." Birch bark stored in carefully wrapped rolls was also found at Star Carr.

Prehistoric chisels and spear points are fascinating and instructive objects, and it is surprisingly exciting to see a collection of needles, awls, fishhooks, axes, and scrapers that came from the workshops of ten thousand years ago. Yet these are all sober workaday things connected with the everlasting struggle to keep fed and clothed. The prehistoric finds that stir the deepest feelings in us are those that hint at the inner life of ancient man—his art, his religion, his personality. That is why the cave paintings of Lascaux and Altamira are so thrilling; that is why a bit of engraved bone rouses more wonder than a hundred flint knives; that is why we feel a shiver of awe at the Venus of Willendorf or even at the necklace of bone beads that lies with a skeleton in some prehistoric grave. Star Carr, too, produced an object of this sort, a haunting and strange Maglemosean relic.

It is the front of the skull of a red deer, with the antlers attached. Both skull and antlers have been pared down and hollowed out, so they form a kind of horned mask. Two eyeholes have been pierced in the lower part of the skull. Was this the headdress of some Maglemosean sorcerer, who wore it while performing a rite designed to bring prosperity to the settlement? A Magdalenian cave painting shows a weird figure crowned with reindeer antlers, surely a tribal medicine man; and this horned mask of ten thousand years ago is perhaps the badge of office of some later representative of the same cult. In shameless imagination we can look across time to a moonlit night by the lakeside, and see the shadowy horned figure leaping and capering to the rhythmic thump of a deer-hide drum. (*Photograph, page viii.*)

Of course, the explanation of the odd mask may be a more earthbound one. Grahame Clark suggests that such masks were worn by hunters in the forest in an attempt to disguise themselves as stags. Not sorcerer's garb, in that case, but clever camouflage. Still, the mask tells us something of its maker.

# 8
# THE
# KITCHEN
# MIDDENS

The Danes have a word for it: *kjøkkenmødding*.

A *kjøkkenmødding*, in English, is a "kitchen midden." A midden is a trash heap, and a kitchen midden is a trash heap of kitchen refuse. The Kitchen Midden Folk of seven thousand years ago did not really have kitchens, but they had plenty of refuse, and they left it all for us to contemplate. Many an archaeologist has passed a dreary summer poking through the debris dumped by these seashore dwellers. It is not the most pleasant work in the world, but out of such chores comes our knowledge of mankind's past.

The middens began piling up because the Maglemoseans, after thousands of years of highly successful existence, found that they could no longer cope with their forest environment. Northern Europe had grown steadily warmer, and the amount of rainfall had notably increased. That had encouraged the rise of a new population of forest trees. At the outset of Maglemosean times, ten thousand years ago, the forests had consisted of straight, slender birches and willows. A man could hunt in such a forest with ease. The later spread of pine trees did not hamper hunting much. But now gigantic oaks filled the woods, surrounded by a dense undergrowth of hazels and alders. Even with their axes, the Maglemoseans could not begin to clear paths through these tangled thickets. Finding and pursuing the deer now became impossible tasks. Crowded out of their forests by the flourishing trees, the Maglemoseans were forced to settle along the seacoast and collect oysters and other shellfish as their main source of food. The oysters were plentiful, but it takes a great many oysters to satisfy a man's appetite. The seashore people devoured multitudes of oysters, and tossed the discarded shells on trash heaps near the settlements— forming the kitchen middens that archaeologists have come to fear and revere. Monumental towers of oyster shells accumulated, thousands of tons of trash. Also thrown into the middens were the other discards of the community, the broken tools and weapons, the objects that tell archaeologists what a culture was like. To find these, they must pick their way through endless millions of oyster shells.

There are hundreds of kitchen middens in Denmark alone. The Danish middens came to the attention of archaeologists long before any of the prehistoric cultures we have been discussing had been rediscovered. As far back as 1837, some learned Danes had poked through a shell heap in the northwest part of the peninsula of Jutland, and had found some flint blades and fragments of worked antler. These had gone to the big National Museum in Copenhagen, where they were filed with thousands of items just like them, and forgotten. A few years later, a Danish zoology professor named Japetus Steenstrup began to study the shell heaps. What interested him was the fact that they all were found a fair distance inland, and so must have been deposited at a time when the shoreline lay in a different place. Steenstrup located about twenty of the heaps on the northern coast of Denmark. In 1848, he reported on his findings to the Danish Academy of Sciences. They were, he said, the remains of oyster beds that had existed when the sea level was much higher than at present—long ago, during the Stone Age. He had concluded this because he had discovered a number of primitive stone tools while exploring the shell deposits.

The mention of stone tools caught the attention of Jens Worsaae, an archaeologist in the audience who held the official title of Inspector of Ancient Monuments. Worsaae, the first full-time government-supported archaeologist in history, suggested to Steenstrup that they return to the shell heaps together and carry out more detailed investigations. Steenstrup agreed; and their interest rose when they heard of the discoveries recently made by road-construction men in northeastern Jutland. Digging into a thick layer of oyster shells to use as surfacing material, the workmen found flint implements and an attractive comb of bone. These antiquities found their way to Worsaae in Copenhagen.

Worsaae was cautious. Though all sorts of obviously man-made material had come from the shell heaps, including potsherds, or bits of broken pottery, he jumped to no conclusions. Even after five days of digging, he would commit himself to nothing more than a wary guess: "One might almost be tempted to believe that this had been a sort of eating place for the people of the neighborhood in the earliest prehistoric times. This would account for the ashes, the bones, the flints and the potsherds. But this is hardly more than a guess, scarcely to be taken seriously."

Some more work strengthened his opinions. By the end of 1850, Worsaae was certain that the shell heaps were artificial—kitchen middens, in fact, the dumping-grounds of early man. In this he disagreed with Steenstrup, who thought that the shell mounds were the remains of oyster banks, or else accumulations that had washed up on shore, and that the human artifacts in them had been dropped there by chance.

On a windswept Danish beach at Christmas time, Worsaae and Steenstrup debated the point at a newly discovered mound, and Steenstrup was converted by Worsaae's reasoning. The heaps, he agreed, were kitchen middens. Since nothing was known at the time of the earlier Maglemosean culture, Worsaae and his colleagues believed that the middens had been deposited by the first inhabitants of Denmark. With great enthusiasm they set to work systematically exploring the middens.

Though they dug in many places, one site in particular has been chosen as typical of the Kitchen Midden culture. This is the midden of Ertebølle, midway across the northern coast of the peninsula of Jutland. The Kitchen Midden culture is therefore known to prehistorians as the Ertebølle culture. (The Danish letter ø is pronounced like the German letter ü—an "oe" or "eh" sound.)

The Ertebølle culture was really a continuation of the Maglemosean, and it preserved many of the ways of the forest society. Now, though, the seashore was the dwelling place. Inland lay thick, impassable forests of oak and linden and elm. In the shelter of these big trees thrived the forest animals, the red deer and roe deer, the wild boar, the wild ox. The Ertebølle men still hunted these animals, but they did not pursue them very far into the woods. It was safer to remain near the shoreside settlement.

What that settlement looked like we cannot certainly say. No traces of Ertebølle houses have been uncovered. Perhaps the Kitchen Midden Folk lived in flimsy shelters of branches, or tents of skins, which would have left no traces for archaeologists. Not even their clothing is known to us, for the sites have yielded no buttons or pins or buckles. We can guess, though, that a camp of these people consisted of a few dozen rough shelters built on top of a long uneven mound beside a beach. To one side—the downwind side of the camp—the mound grew steadily, for all the refuse of the camp was dumped there. Dogs, an important part of the life of the settlement, rooted in this kitchen midden, hunting for stray scraps of meat on bones.

It was a busy community, everyone with his assigned task. The gathering of food was the main responsibility. There was as yet no farming, no raising of livestock. Food had to be found the hard way, by hunting or by collecting it in the wilds. While the men, armed with bows and arrows, ranged the borders of the forest in quest of game, children and old people waded in the sea at low tide to harvest oysters and other shellfish. Boats of fishermen went out regularly to cast their nets and lines. Hunters with harpoons sometimes killed the seals of the coastal waters. The flocks of birds that soared overhead were regularly thinned by expert marksmen using sharp, flint-tipped arrows.

Behind the hunters lay the vital work of the craftsmen who provided the artillery. Bows and arrows, harpoons of bone, butchering axes of deer antler and flint, spears, nets, fishhooks—all these things had to come from the workshops of the settlement. Stone

*124*    tools were made in the ancient tried-and-true way, by chipping flakes from cores of flint, but a new method also emerged among these Kitchen Midden people. They used stones other than flint, such as granite, which could not be split easily. To shape them, they pounded or "pecked" them to the desired form, getting them to an approximately satisfactory shape that way and then grinding and polishing them until they were sharp. It seems like a small thing, this shift from chipped flint tools to pecked granite ones, but actually it marks a major breakaway from Old Stone Age techniques. Ever since those remote days when the men of a million years ago had clumsily banged two stones together until they had something that could be used as an axe, tools had been fashioned by essentially the same method. The method had grown ever more refined, of course, culminating in the subtle and superb Solutrean blades. But it was still basically just the chipping of stone, however beautifully it was done.

Now, though, these Mesolithic people of the northern coasts were grinding and polishing at least some of their implements. That was a slower, more taxing process, indicating an attitude of patience that showed mankind settling down. A skilled craftsman could turn out a wonderfully elegant flint blade in a matter of hours; but to grind an axe to shape required days of work and a sort of determination that must have been rare in Ice Age man.

The distinction between chipped blades and polished ones seemed so important to the prehistorians of the nineteenth century that they used it as the dividing point for an entire era. So it is that we have the terms "Paleolithic" and "Neolithic." The Neolithic, or New Stone Age, was the name given to the era in which polished stone tools became widespread. Actually, as we will see, a much more important difference separates the Old Stone Age from the New. But we continue to use the earlier system of names based on the method of fashioning stone tools.

The Ertebølle folk belong to the Mesolithic, the time of transition between Paleolithic and Neolithic. They used both methods of making stone tools. Archaeologists have suggested that the development of polished stone implements grew out of the use of bone tools, which began in Aurignacian times. Bone cannot be chipped or retouched, but must be ground, cut, or polished into shape. Familiarity with these techniques of working bone may have led some Mesolithic cultures to experiment with preparing stone the same way, especially in regions where easily fractured stone such as flint was not available.

From the kitchen middens, also, came another novelty: the earliest northern European pottery. Far away in the Near East, vessels of clay had been in use for a long time, but we have no reason to think that there was any direct contact between Mesopotamia and Denmark seven thousand years ago. The invention of pottery on the shores of the Baltic Sea was probably achieved independently.

There is a possibility that the Magdalenian peoples of Belgium made some rough unbaked vessels out of raw clay about sixteen thousand years ago. However, no true pottery has been found in any northern European sites before Ertebølle times. The discovery may have been an accident. Possibly the Ertebølle women had taken to shaping soft storage vessels out of clay. Then, one day, such a vessel fell into a fire, and when it was taken out it was found to be much harder, practically like stone. Centuries of experimentation eventually led to a reliable method for making sturdy pottery: finding good clay, mixing it with sand or powdered rock to give it toughness,

126 shaping it into bowls and jars, heating it to just the
right temperature. Too much heat and the vessel
would crack; too little, and it would not be durable.
The result was the dark-hued, baggy, pointy-
bottomed Ertebølle pottery the fragments of which
are so common in the Danish kitchen middens.

Kitchen Midden pottery would win no beauty
prizes in a ceramics exhibition. It is gloomy looking,
lumpy stuff. But it played a key role in the revolution
of daily existence that was just gathering force.
Pottery offered new opportunities. Seeds and nuts
could now be stored safely where rodents could not
reach them. Stews, porridges, and soups could be
added to the diet. Certain plants that could not be
eaten unless boiled now became staples of the meal.
Cooking food was no longer a complex business that
involved dropping red-hot stones into leather vessels
of water; it was relatively simple to set a clay pot of
water to boil over a fire.

Because of such humble achievements—clumsy
pots, polished stone blades, the use of the bow and
arrow, the taming of the dog—we set these Mesolithic folk of the north down as trail blazers. They
hold no real glamour for us otherwise. The eaters of
oysters do not stir our imaginations the way the men
of the Ice Age do. We respond with a tingle of excitement to the image of Aurignacian hunters setting
out over an icy wasteland to do battle with the
woolly mammoth, or to the picture of Magdalenian
artists painting masterpieces on the walls of dank,
dark caves. We cannot respond in quite the same
way to these later people, living quietly in their sea-
side huts atop vast mounds of discarded rubbish.
Yet they are far closer in spirit to ourselves than are
the storm-raked cave dwellers of the Paleolithic.
They are on their way toward becoming town
dwellers, farmers, citizens. They look humdrum be-

side their rugged ancestors; but doubtless they regarded themselves as remarkably progressive, highly
advanced, the vanguard of civilization.

Though they probably had no way of knowing it,
the Ertebølle people were progressive and advanced
only by European standards of the time. In other
parts of the world, particularly the Near East, the
pace of progress had been more swift. In Upper
Paleolithic times, western Europe had been a fertile
source of new ideas, virtually the intellectual capital
of the Ice Age world. Now, though, the center of
progress had shifted elsewhere. Europe had become
a backwoods region of cultural laggards, a state of
affairs not destined to change for thousands of years.

The big news from the Near East was the shift
from food gathering to food producing. This wholesale change in the human economy is known as the
Neolithic revolution. It was marked by many technical advances—such as the change from chipped
stone tools to polished stone tools that gave the
period its name—but the real and overwhelming
basis of the revolution lay in the new ways of obtaining food.

Before the Neolithic Period, man was dependent
on what nature provided for food, shelter, and clothing. The best he could do to improve his lot was to
design more efficient hunting weapons. Eventually,
the food supply in a given region became too scanty
to support human life, and he had to move along.
The nomad life did not encourage great cultural
advances. Possessions had to be kept at a minimum
so the tribe could travel light. Small children were
a handicap. When man lived by hunting and fishing
alone, he was condemned to exist in sparse groups
that had little material wealth.

Some nine or ten thousand years ago, certain
human groups took the giant step toward independ-

*128*   ence. They learned how to grow crops and how to domesticate livestock. They discovered that useful grains like wheat and barley could be raised by planting seeds in cultivated soil, and by watering and weeding and tending. They found out how to make sturdy, watertight pottery vessels. They learned that wild pigs and sheep and cattle could be tamed and kept close at hand to serve as permanent sources of meat and milk. Settlements of a lasting nature sprang up next to the best grazing and farming lands. The first villages were born. The new ease of obtaining food permitted a sudden and dramatic expansion of population. A flood of new inventions followed—the house, the loom, the plough, the sickle, and many others. Life was totally transformed.

The first centers of Neolithic life were in Syria, Palestine, and Iraq. Though we are not sure where the revolution actually began, the evidence at present points to the valley of the Jordan River. Excavations at the city of Jericho, in what is now the Kingdom of Jordan, have yielded carbon-14 dates of eighty-eight hundred years ago for an early Neolithic settlement. Even that long ago, Jericho was a large fortified town covering at least eight acres, with a population of as many as three thousand, engaged in the raising of crops and the domestication of animals. Beyond a doubt the first settlements at Jericho go back several thousand years before that.

At a time when the Maglemosean huntsmen were preying on forest deer, Jericho and its neighboring towns were already well into the Neolithic. Yet the Maglemoseans were the most advanced culture of Europe. By 5000 B.C., when the Kitchen Midden camps were being founded, Jericho was an ancient city, and the Neolithic revolution had spread into Iran and North Africa. The future great civilizations of Egypt and Mesopotamia were beginning to take

shape at a time when in Europe's most advanced *129*
culture men were just starting to learn how to make
clay pottery.

The new ideas spread slowly into Europe. Out of
the sunlit lands of Syria the word traveled to the
islands of the eastern Mediterranean, such as Crete
and Malta, and then leaped to the European mainland. Archaeologists are just beginning now to trace
the route of Neolithic ways as they entered Europe.
An important discovery was made in 1961 in Greece
by a young American archaeologist named Robert J.
Rodden.

Rodden had gone to England to do advanced work
at the University of Cambridge. His interest in early
Neolithic times led him to explore the Macedonian
plain of northern Greece, which is marked by the
low-lying mounds that hide the remains of ancient
settlements. One mound in particular had come to
the attention of archaeologists in 1958 when the bull-
dozers of road builders split it open, revealing
pottery and other artifacts. In 1960 Rodden paid a
visit to this mound, at a village called Nea Nikomedeia, and recognized its importance. The following year he returned to excavate. He was accompanied by Grahame Clark of Cambridge, who had
earlier worked on the Star Carr Maglemosean settlement in England.

Six weeks of excavation in 1961 produced rich
layers of early Neolithic material, including pottery
fragments, animal bones, the foundations of mud-
walled houses, and the imprints of wheat grains.
When a carbon-14 dating showed an age of eight
thousand years for this settlement, Rodden and Clark
knew that they had uncovered the oldest known
Neolithic settlement of Europe. Returning in 1963,
they embarked on a full-scale excavation that lasted
four months. The archaeologists painstakingly

130  scraped away the earth, laying bare the Neolithic levels over an area of half an acre.

They uncovered a number of houses that had been built beside a marshy lake no longer in existence. They were one-room dwellings made of oak frames plastered with mud. There was evidence that the Nea Nikomedeia farmers had raised wheat, barley, and lentils, and had kept herds of sheep and goats, with smaller numbers of cattle and pigs. "In addition to tending their flocks," Rodden wrote, "the people of Nea Nikomedeia engaged in hunting, fowling, and fishing. Deer, hare, and wild pig were among the game animals; the presence of fish bones and the shells of both saltwater cockles and freshwater mussels shows that the early settlers also exploited the resources of their coastal environment."

These Greek settlers may have come from Syria or Asia Minor to found a Neolithic colony on the European mainland. Or perhaps they were natives of the region who learned from travelers about the revolutionary developments to the east. It seems more likely that these early European farmers were immigrants from overseas than that they sprang from the old hunting cultures. Archaeologists now are recovering the traces of a large influx of Neolithic people into Europe from abroad. They moved into a continent that was nearly empty, inhabited only by wandering tribes of Mesolithic hunters. The Mesolithic peoples watched the newcomers building their farming settlements, and gradually came to imitate them.

Two main thrusts of this peaceful invasion have been outlined. One group of Neolithic colonists spread northward out of Asia Minor and Syria. They entered Europe through Bulgaria and northern Greece, and plunged onward along the valley of the Danube River until eventually they reached Scandinavia. The Nea Nikomedeia settlement represents one of the early colonies along this eastern route.

The other path was a sea route westward through the Mediterranean, from the Greek islands to Malta and Sicily, into southern Italy, then to the south of France and the east coast of Spain. There the western Neolithic folk turned north toward the British Isles.

There is no reason to think that there was war between the established Mesolithic tribes of Europe and these two columns of Neolithic colonists. The Mesolithic people were so few in number that they must simply have given way to the vigorous newcomers without a struggle.

The Neolithic settlements of southwest Asia thus set in motion a great tide of cultural colonization. As the British archaeologist Jacquetta Hawkes puts it, the Neolithic area of Asia "can be seen as the heart of the Old World, pumping out pulses of cultural energy through the continents." It was not a rapid outward movement, though. Generation by generation, the emigrants from Asia Minor and Syria cleared the forests of Europe, built new towns, prospered and multiplied—and then sent pioneers onward, searching for lands where they could repeat the process. So one wave moved from island to island along the Mediterranean coast, and the other moved from valley to valley across the heart of Europe. We can picture the older populations hearing of the villagers first from third-hand reports, then getting a more detailed account as the Neolithic zone came nearer to their own territory. It must have been humbling to the Ertebølle folk and other Mesolithic peoples to discover that they were not the summit of human endeavor after all, but merely rude backwoodsmen of no particular importance.

Danish archaeologists have done the most to reveal this collision of cultures. Careful study of the kitchen middens has shown the nature of the impact of the farmers on the Ertebølle people. It was about five thousand years ago that the Neolithic settlers of the Danube-following group finally reached Denmark, by way of Poland and Germany. For several hundred years, it seems, the native hunters and the Neolithic farmers lived peacefully side by side. This is indicated by the presence of various Neolithic items in the Kitchen Midden deposits. The Ertebølle people went on living more or less as they always had, and even grew more flourishing, increasing their numbers and building new settlements.

This apparently puzzling late prosperity of the Kitchen Midden Folk was possibly an indirect boon from the newcomers. The latter were busily clearing the virgin forests to make room for their own fields and pastures, and this allowed the Ertebølle hunters more easily to reach the deer that they depended on for their meat supply. Eventually, though, the farmers were so numerous that the forests were virtually destroyed, and the people of the older culture no longer could survive as hunters. Some migrated to the untouched woods of the far north; some adapted to Neolithic ways, and melted into the farming population. In that way the Mesolithic cultures of Europe slowly disappeared.

How the Neolithic farmers managed to clear the European forests with their flint axes was long a mystery to archaeology. It seemed impossible that such inefficient tools could chop down the mighty oaks that covered most of northern Europe five thousand years ago. In 1952, two Danish archaeologists began an interesting series of experiments that revealed how it was accomplished.

The archaeologists, Svend Jørgenson and Jørgen Troels-Smith, borrowed actual Neolithic flint axe blades from the National Museum in Copenhagen

and mounted them on wooden hafts modeled after
an actual ancient axe preserved in a Danish bog.
Then, accompanied by two professional lumberjacks,
they went to work on some sturdy oaks in a nearby
forest.

They quickly learned that the usual tree-chopping
method of long, powerful blows of the axe would not
work at all. The flint blades simply shattered. But by

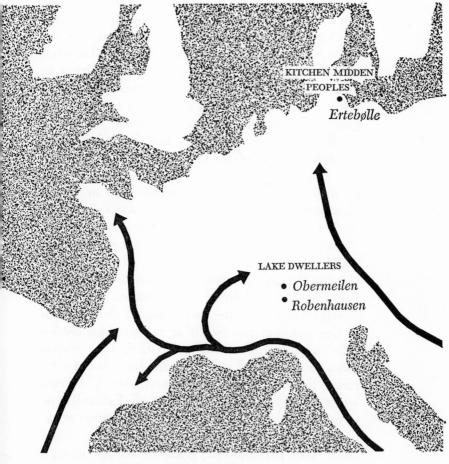

KITCHEN MIDDEN
PEOPLES

*Ertebølle*

LAKE DWELLERS
• *Obermeilen*
• *Robenhausen*

EARLY NEOLITHIC MIGRATIONS

*134*   chipping at the trees with short, quick strokes, using mainly the elbow and wrist, they were able to cut down foot-thick oak trees in half an hour. The experiment proved that Neolithic man could have cleared large forest areas quickly with his seemingly primitive tools.

Next the Danish researchers set out to find how the cleared land was made suitable for planting. It seemed likely that the stumps and felled trees had been removed by fire. In May 1954 the archaeologists burned off the clearing making use of a method employed in backward parts of Finland until quite recently. They spread dry brushwood and branches over a one-acre plot and used birchbark torches to light the fire. When the blaze was well along, they pushed burning logs with long poles toward those that had not yet caught fire. "In this way we burned off the tangle of vegetation belt by belt," wrote Johannes Iversen of the University of Copenhagen, who took part in the work. "The fire was controlled carefully, day and night, to achieve an even and thorough burning of the ground. It was rather hard work, as oak wood burns slowly, but there were no serious difficulties, and in three or four days the job was finished. We burned only half of the two-acre clearing, because we wished to compare the subsequent growth on burned and unburned ground."

After the burning, the archaeologists planted seeds of the sort that the Neolithic farmers had used— primitive forms of wheat and barley. They spread them on the ground and scratched them under with forked branches. "On the unburned ground," Iversen wrote, "the grain scarcely grew at all. Evidently the rather acid forest soil was not suited to cereal growing. But the burned ground produced a luxuriant crop." They harvested the grain Neolithic style, with a flint knife and a flint sickle.

With such methods—slashing and burning—the *135*
Neolithic farmers of Europe cut down the great
forests and turned them into fields and pastures.
Pockets of hunters still remained, of course, in regions where the farmers had not yet penetrated. But
the Neolithic revolution was spreading swiftly. The
day of the wandering hunters was nearly over.

# 9
# THE LAKE
# DWELLERS

While one column of Neolithic settlers was making its gradual way across eastern Europe toward Germany and Scandinavia, a parallel movement was under way in western Europe. These western Neolithic peoples had traveled the length of the Mediterranean before turning inland through France and Spain. Originally, perhaps, they came from Syria and Asia Minor, but they were joined at some point by another stream from North Africa.

Up they moved through territory that had been the heartland of the Aurignacians and Magdalenians thousands of years before. Those sturdy cave dwellers had long since been forgotten, of course. As far as the pioneer farmers were concerned, Spain and France had never been settled before. The scattered bands of hunters and fishers—descendants of

138 the Azilian pebble-painters and other early Mesolithic folk—were so sparse as to be practically invisible.

Onward the farmers came, building their villages, clearing the forests, raising their crops, tending their herds. They cultivated the olive and the grape. They knew how to spin and weave. They made good pottery. They had excellent stone tools, carefully ground and polished to a keen edge. As they moved northward, they split into several groups. One turned eastward out of France, heading across Germany toward land already occupied by the eastern Neolithic people. One turned westward, through Brittany toward England.

The main body of these western Neolithic folk moved generally northward across the Alps into Switzerland. They built villages there of an unusual and distinctive kind, by the shores of lakes in whose cool waters snow-capped mountains were reflected. In time, those villages were abandoned and vanished from the memory of man. Then, in the middle of the nineteenth century, they were discovered anew.

In 1853 Switzerland experienced an unusually cold, dry winter. Little snow fell, and spring was late in 1854, so that the mountain streams did not produce the usual bounty of the thaw. The rivers that feed Switzerland's lakes were starved for water, and the level of the lakes themselves dropped sharply. Lake Zurich in particular suffered. The shoreline shrank inward, exposing great stretches of rocky beach that had not been laid bare for as long as anyone could remember.

Farmers who owned property along the Swiss lakes shrewdly set about making their gains of land permanent. They built stone dikes along the new borders of the lakes, and dredged up lake-bottom mud to use as fill for the reclaimed area. When the water level rose again, the lakes would not be able to return to their old boundaries, and the new land, safe behind the retaining walls of stone, could be farmed.

The workmen who were filling in the shoreline at Obermeilen and Dollikon, on the north side of Lake Zurich, ran into an unexpected difficulty when they attempted to dredge up mud for the fill. When their spades got a foot or so below the muddy surface, they struck something solid. The puzzled workmen found row upon row of stout wooden beams, four to six inches thick and three to five feet long. These beams, or piles, had been sharpened at one end and driven vertically into the mud at distances of about a foot from each other. This forest of wooden piles covered a wide zone stretching 1,200 feet along the shore and extending out toward the deep water.

The presence of the piles made the dredging job an extremely difficult one. But it had to be done before the overdue spring thaw arrived and put an end to the reclamation project. Grumbling a little, the workmen started to dredge mud from between the piles. All sorts of objects came up with the mud: a great many antlers, and tools fashioned from bone and stone, and then an extraordinary bronze axe head. This trove of ancient treasure came to the attention of Johannes Aeppli of the town of Obermeilen, who recognized its importance. He sent word to the Zurich Antiquarian Society, and before long the president of that society, Dr. Ferdinand Keller, was making the six-mile journey from Zurich to Obermeilen.

Keller was regarded as one of Switzerland's foremost archaeologists. However, archaeology in 1854 was a part-time profession for most people, and

*140* Keller's main field of study was quite different; he was a professor of English literature. Now fifty-three years old, he had devoted the last twenty of those years to a systematic archaeological exploration of the region about Zurich.

The Zurich Antiquarian Society began speedily to collect artifacts from the lake site, under Keller's direction. They found many flat bronze axes, finely

*Tools and implements from the Swiss Lake Dwellings: axes, chisels and awls, kitchen utensils and carvings.*

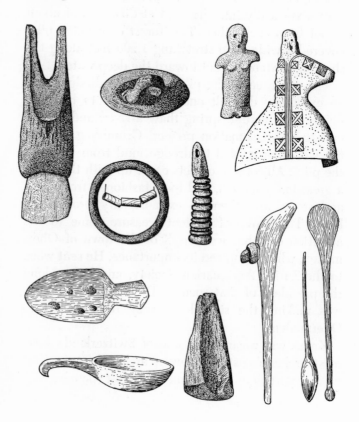

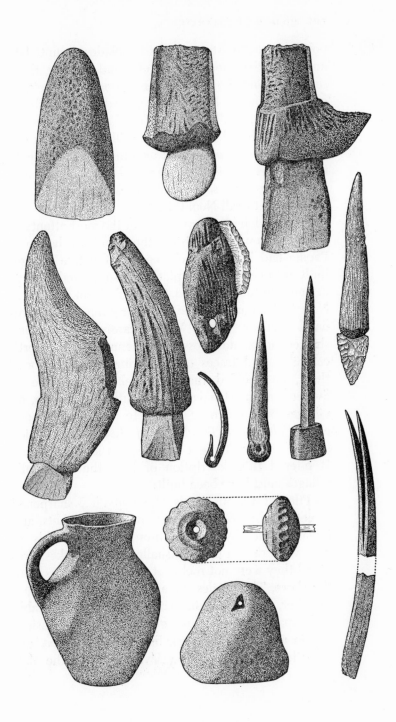

142 polished axes of stone, and flint blades mounted in antler handles. Pieces of basketry and matting, thousands of animal bones, fragments of pottery of several qualities, amber beads, knives and awls made of boar's teeth, mallets made from antlers, grinding stones that had been used for milling grain, sickles and saws of stone, all this and much else came to the surface. Obviously there had been a rich and complex ancient settlement here, of the kind we have come to call Neolithic.

The wooden piles, however, got the most attention.

Explorers who had visited the islands of the South Pacific had brought back reports of native villages built out over water on platforms supported by logs driven into the water bed. These platform villages of New Guinea and Borneo were very much on Ferdinand Keller's mind. When careful examination showed horizontal crossbeams connecting the vertical piles, and traces of a flooring platform above them, he decided that the prehistoric people of Switzerland must have lived, South Sea fashion, on villages built out over lakes. He published a book called *The Lake Dwellings of Switzerland* which stirred wide excitement in European learned circles. It offered this description of how the Swiss pile villages must have been built:

"Piles of various kinds of wood . . . sharpened sometimes by fire, sometimes by stone hatchets, and in later times by tools of bronze and probably of iron, were driven into the shallows of the lakes, provided they were not rocky, at various distances from the shore. These piles were placed sometimes close together, sometimes in pairs, sometimes tolerably wide apart—generally in regular order, but occasionally in apparent confusion. In all cases the heads of the piles were brought to a level, and then the platform beams were laid upon them. . . . Occasionally cross timbers were joined to the upright piles below the platform to support and steady the structure, either forced in, as it were, between them, or fastened to them by what workmen call 'notching,' that is, portions were cut out of the vertical piles to receive the cross timbers. The platform lying on the top of this series of piles appears in many cases to have been of the rudest construction, and to have consisted merely of one or two layers of unbarked stems lying parallel one to another."

The drought of 1853–54 had come at a perfect time—a time of great interest in archaeology all over Europe. Keller's book found a fascinated audience, and other archaeologists began searching for pile villages on the shores of the lakes of Switzerland and northern Italy. They found them by the dozens. From places called Robenhausen and Mooseedorf and Nidau-Steinberg and Maurach came news of more beds of piles, and such a torrent of antiquities that the museums of Switzerland were flooded with them.

One of the most fertile sources of Lake Dweller artifacts was Robenhausen, on the lake of Pfäffikon near Zurich. In January 1858 a studious farmhand named Jakob Messikommer, who was well aware of Keller's discoveries, found the Robenhausen settlement while cutting peat. Messikommer dug his way through marshy ground south of the lake, and came upon a village covering some 120,000 square feet and built on 100,000 piles. The layer of artifacts was a yard thick, and kept Messikommer busy excavating there for the next fifty years. It was slow, unpleasant work—he had to stake out small areas of the marsh and pump them dry—but it yielded an immense fund of Lake Dweller relics. Messikommer became an

*144*  expert archaeologist as he worked, and was able to distinguish several different villages that had been built on the site over perhaps a thousand years. He supported his work by selling his surplus artifacts to European museums, so that eventually no self-respecting museum was complete without a Lake Dweller display supplied by the indefatigable Messi-kommer.

Ferdinand Keller, too, continued to work on the pile villages. His office in Zurich became the central clearing house for Lake Dweller data, and his reports grew ever more bulky, so that the 1878 edition of *The Lake Dwellings of Switzerland* filled two fat volumes and described hundreds of sites. Until his death in 1881 Keller labored to bring order out of this vast mass of material and present a clear picture of what the Lake Dweller culture was like.

Keller drew a complete and convincing portrait of his Lake Dwellers, and backed it up with scale models and elaborate reconstructions. He told of parties of pioneers pushing through the forests to the lake shores, two or three hundred people, perhaps, carrying with them a few bags of seed corn and driving a handful of cattle and sheep along. The first year of settlement was a busy one. While dwelling in temporary shelters on the beach, the new-comers set about the task of clearing the surrounding forests for agriculture. Polished flint axes sent mighty trees crashing to the ground; then the trunks and branches were split and cut into piles and hauled down to the water's edge. While one party of work-men pounded the piles into the mud, another carried out the job of burning off the clearing. Crops were planted; grazing land was staked out for the herds. Meanwhile the foundations for the lake dwelling were securely fastened in place and the cross timbers lashed or notched to the vertical piles. Next, the platform was woven across the top of this foundation of piles, which now stood several feet above the surface of the lake.

By autumn the platform was finished and the first houses were being built—simple one-or-two-roomed dwellings whose walls were of wooden stakes plastered with mud, and whose roofs were thatched with rushes. The villagers celebrated their first harvest festival in their new homes. As winter closed in, they carefully stored seeds and grain in clay jars until spring.

Now the community had taken root and its real growth could begin. Year after year, the clearing of the forest proceeded, and new platforms were built, extending ever farther into the water. The herds grew bigger, for the villagers knew the secret of slaughtering for meat only those animals that were not needed for bearing offspring. The fields now yielded a variety of crops: wheat and barley, peas and beans and lentils, plums and apples, flax and berries. The women tended the fields, weeding and hoeing, using flint sickles to reap at harvest time. It was a lively farming community, with plenty of work for all. The grinding of meal, the baking of bread, the weaving of clothes, the making of tools, the milking of cows, and dozens of other chores kept old and young active. Sudden catastrophe might interrupt the pleasant round of industry, though—a fire, perhaps, sweeping through the wooden houses, or a terrible storm that whipped the lake to fury and ripped the platforms apart. Then would come a time of rebuilding and steady effort to regain the prosperity that had been lost.

That was Ferdinand Keller's picture of life among the Lake Dwellers five thousand years ago. He based it strictly on the archaeological record, and it still stands as a substantially accurate view of life in a Neolithic community of Europe. Only one facet of Keller's reconstruction of Lake Dweller life has been challenged by later researchers, and that is nothing less than the basic concept of the settlements themselves. The whole notion of prehistoric villages built out on piles over lakes, which enthralled prehistorians for more than a hundred years, has been overthrown.

Keller had his opponents right from the outset. Even before the appearance of Keller's first report, another Swiss archaeologist named Albert Jahn had offered a different interpretation of the pile fields. Jahn felt that the piles did represent the foundations of prehistoric villages, but that the villages had risen by the shores of lakes, not *in* the lakes. The foundations now were submerged, Jahn said, because the lakes had grown larger in recent centuries, covering the ancient shores.

The more romantic Keller theory, with its echoes of the platform villages of the South Seas, won wide support, and Jahn's ideas were ignored. One school of German archaeologists remained concerned with what they called "the pile-dwelling problem." They were convinced that the villages had been built on low-lying swampy ground, not over water. One of them, Hans Reinerth, carried out studies along the shores of Lake Constance in the 1920's that seriously questioned the truth of Keller's findings. More recent excavations seemingly have dealt the deathblow to the picturesque old theory.

One of these expeditions was sponsored by the Bern Historical Museum in 1957, under the leadership of a young archaeologist named Hansjürgen Müller-Beck. Müller-Beck worked by the shores of

the Swiss lake of Burgäschi, where four separate Neolithic settlements had been discovered. One of these,
on the south shore of the little lake, proved particularly fruitful.

No piles were visible above the surface of the lake,
nor along the beach. In the fifty centuries since the
abandonment of the village, a thick layer of soil and
sediment had covered the foundation piles. More
than three thousand piles were uncovered, though,
made from the trunks of ash, alder, and young oak
trees. The settlers, according to Müller-Beck, had
occupied the site about a hundred years. "When they
arrived," he wrote, "they found a broad and treeless
strip of land that was ideal for cultivation. The lake,
of moderate size when it was formed in the last Ice
Age, had been gradually retreating, leaving on its
shores mollusk shells and the deposits of carbon and
lime that form around the roots of water plants. The
soil cover was still too light to permit trees to take
root and grow, but it was quite heavy enough for the
demands of primitive agriculture."

Though the beach area was perfect for farming,
thanks to the fertile deposits of mud and minerals
left behind by the retreating lake, it was not so
suitable as a place to live. The soil was soggy and
weak, and could not support the weight of houses
built in a conventional manner. As foundations for
their houses, the settlers laid down a floor of rubble,
branches, and earth, which they pounded firm. Then
they made this floor secure by driving wooden piles
through it and through the swampy ground below,
into the gravel bedrock that underlay the boglike
beach.

Even this anchored floor, apparently, did not entirely meet the need. "It is clear," wrote Müller-Beck,
"that the settlement was often in need of repair. The

*148*  floors sank in the middle as the earth beneath them gave way. For a while they could be leveled by the addition of new layers of rubble, branches, and loam. ... But eventually more drastic action became necessary and the entire settlement had to be moved a few feet back from the lake, onto drier land." The archaeologist found the successive sets of piles that marked these moves back from the shore.

The final settlement was about fifty yards long and ten yards wide, enclosed by a palisade fence except on the side facing the lake. Log roads anchored on piles ran from house to house inside the palisade. Within the fence were three buildings, two dwellings and one that might have been a stable or a granary. A rubbish heap nearby revealed that the villagers had still depended to some extent on hunting; the bones of wild animals such as boar, beaver, fox, deer, and bear were found beside those of the domesticated pig, goat, sheep, and dog. Grain and flax were raised, but mushrooms, hazelnuts, and wild berries were gathered as well. So these lake people, although farmers, did not ignore the food sources of the Mesolithic hunting and gathering folk.

The site yielded stone axes and knives, flint arrowheads, bone chisels and awls, harpoons and drinking cups of deer horn. Well preserved in the wet, airless bog were wooden implements: clubs, lances, drills used for making fire, the handles of tools, and even an arrowshaft with a stone arrowhead still in place.

As at most Lake Dweller sites, objects of metal were also found. The presence of copper or bronze artifacts in a Neolithic village shows that there was no really abrupt break between the Stone Age and the Bronze Age that followed it. When man first learned how to make use of metals, it did not seem to him like the revolutionary step it actually was.

Metals were scarce, hard to refine and work, and not as useful for heavy-duty tools as trusty old stone. They served only for special tools, ornaments, and weapons of the wealthy; the ordinary peasants continued for centuries to use flint knives, axes, and hoes. So while metal eventually replaced stone entirely as the tool material, that development was slow in coming.

Copper and gold were man's first metals. They occur in pure metallic form, and do not necessarily have to be extracted from mineral ores. Stone Age man, discovering nuggets or lumps of these metals, found that he could shape them by hammering and cutting. Gold was too soft for practical use, but its gleaming beauty gave it a decorative value it has never lost. Pure copper could be made into daggers, axes, or knives, though it took a poor cutting edge. Eventually, harder kinds of copper were found, naturally mixed with small quantities of nickel, tin, silver, or other minerals. When prehistoric man saw that he could create such alloys himself, by heating pure copper and adding other metals to it, he entered the Age of Bronze.

Bronze, consisting of copper with about a 10 per cent tin content, first was produced in western Asia some six thousand years ago—that is, while Europe was still entirely Mesolithic. The early smiths, through long experimentation, found ways to build charcoal fires hot enough to melt copper and tin. Thus they formed the new alloy, which was not only harder than copper but also easier to melt and cast into useful forms. Syria entered the Bronze Age at least five thousand years ago, and the technique spread to Asia Minor and the Greek islands some centuries later. Europeans did not begin to make their own bronze implements until about four thousand

*150* years ago; but long before that they were buying Asiatic bronze tools and weapons brought to them by traveling merchants. The Lake Dwellers were good customers. The presence of metal goods in their villages provides evidence for a prehistoric trade route linking the simple farmers of inland Europe with the great civilizations south of the Alps. The metalworkers of Crete, Cyprus, Troy, and Syria produced many items that found their way overland to Switzerland in return for the grain and cloth that these frontiersmen could offer as payment.

The work of Hansjürgen Müller-Beck and other modern archaeologists has demonstrated thoroughly that, despite Ferdinand Keller's careful research, Swiss Lake Dwellers never built villages in the water. Microscopic examination of the mud around the pile deposits reveals that it contains land-grown vegetation, not water plants. The Neolithic settlers preferred to live on the moist, swampy shores of the lakes because the shores offered adequate space for villages without the need to clear huge forest areas; but they had to put down foundations of piles to keep their homes from settling into the soft ground.

The new interpretation does not entirely rule out stilt-borne dwellings, though. The early Lake Dweller houses, with their floors against the damp ground, were vulnerable to rotting and to invasion by mice and other vermin. As their skill at carpentry increased, especially after bronze tools came into their hands, the Lake Dwellers learned to raise their houses slightly above the ground by supporting them on piles that projected past the surface. These off-the-ground dwellings would have looked something like those Ferdinand Keller had in mind, except that they stood on the shore.

So the Keller theory has to be scrapped, which

does not in any way detract from the value of his    *151*
archaeological work in general. He guessed wrong
about the location of his pile villages, but through
his tireless labors he recaptured from the mud of the
Swiss lakes an entire culture of early European
farmers.

# THE NEW STONE AGE: NEOLITHIC PERIOD

| 6,000 to 4,000 B.C. | 3,500 to 2000 B.C. |
|---|---|

**EUROPE**

Neolithic farmers migrate through most of Europe.

Lake Dweller villages in Switzerland.

Kitchen Midden and Maglemosean peoples. Polished granite tools, early pottery, fishing, carpentry.

Megalithic cult spreads through western Europe, 3000-1500 B.C.

Neolithic migrations from Asia Minor into Europe begin about 6000 B.C., from Africa slightly later. Earliest known site at Nea Nikomedeia.

Traders from Asia Minor and Crete establish colonies and routes, bring Bronze Age products and Mother Goddess cult to Western Europe. Los Millares in Spain 3500 B.C.

**MEDITERRANEAN**

Settled village life in Asia Minor. Agriculture, pottery, domestic animals.

Bronze produced in Asia Minor 4000 B.C.

Egypt in high civilization. Great pyramids 2700 B.C.

| 2000 to 1000 B.C. | 1000 to 50 B.C. |

Megalith builders in Spain, France, Britain, Scandinavia.

Stonehenge built about 1800 B.C.

Beaker Folk spread Bronze Age culture by trade and colonization from Spain through Europe.

Battle Axe People enter Europe from Russia, spread north and west. Horses and chariots, herding economy, sun-worship, Indo-European languages.

Celtic civilization develops in Europe from mixture of peoples. Bronze Age and early Iron Age cultures.

Halstatt Period 1000-500 B.C.

La Tène Period 500 B.C.

Cretan and Mycenaean civilizations trade by land and sea for European tin, copper, amber, Camonica Valley 2000-500 B.C.

Trade continues between Celtic Europe and the Mediterranean World.

Celts burn Rome 381 B.C.

Iron Age in Asia Minor 1400 B.C.

Trojan War about 1250 B.C.

Egypt at height of her civilization.

Golden age of Greece 500 B.C.

Roman Republic founded 500 B.C.

Julius Caesar conquers Gaul and Britain 50 B.C. Europe enters historic period.

# 10
# DOLMENS
# AND
# MENHIRS

The Neolithic immigrants who entered Europe five thousand years ago settled down to practice their farming skills. But they did not go unvisited. Among them came merchants and missionaries from the wealthy Bronze Age cultures of the east, who brought a new religion and carried their faith to the far corners of Europe. These zealous missionaries converted the heathen frontiersmen of the Neolithic villages, setting in motion a wave of religious passion that lasted more than a thousand years. Or so it seems to us.

We are on shaky ground when we try to comprehend prehistoric religion, since there are no written records. We know a good deal about the faiths of Egypt and Mesopotamia, because those powerful ancient civilizations left us full written accounts. The gods of Egypt are no strangers to us: hawk-headed

*156*     Horus and lion-faced Sekhmet, the falcon Re and the beetle Khepra, the crocodile-god Sobek and the cat-goddess Ubaste. We know the rituals with which they were worshiped; we know the roles they played in Egyptian thought and philosophy. The clay tablets of Sumer and Babylonia reveal the Mesopotamian gods and myths in the same way the coiled rolls of papyrus reveal those of Egypt. We can read the story of the creation of the world, the epic deeds of the hero Gilgamesh, the tale of the war among the gods.

All these things were set down in writing forty centuries ago, and more. During the same period, a vigorous religious movement was sweeping Europe. We do not know the names of its gods. We have no inkling of its mythology. The tablets of Sumer and the papyri of Egypt speak to us in clear voices; but Europe is silent. All we have to mark the existence of this movement, which took hold of the souls of an entire continent, is a series of stone monuments— massive, enigmatic, and voiceless. They are the megaliths of Europe. (*Photographs, pages 193–195.*)

The word "megalith" was coined by archaeologists about the year 1850, and comes from two Greek words, *megas* and *lithos,* meaning "great" and "stone." There are many types of megalithic monuments, but what links them all is the hugeness of the stones from which they were constructed. A megalithic tomb in central France, sixty-one feet long by sixteen feet wide and nine feet high, is roofed by four capstones each about two feet thick that weigh more than eighty tons apiece. A broken megalithic stone in Brittany once was sixty-five feet high. A single stone of an Irish megalithic monument weighs over one hundred tons. For what reason these mighty slabs of stone were jockeyed into their positions, we do not know. But whole populations labored to erect them, driven by some mysterious and powerful impulse that could only have been religious in nature. Like the towering cathedrals of the Middle Ages, the megalithic tombs and temples are the solid evidence of a surging mystic drive.

There are some fifty thousand megalithic monuments in western Europe. Most of them have been known for hundreds of years, for it is hard to overlook a vast ancient monument standing close by a settled area. The superstitious people of medieval times spoke of the megaliths as the work of giants, or perhaps of the devil, since clearly no ordinary force could have raised such colossal blocks of stone. Throughout Europe many of these monuments still bear the names given them by peasants five or ten centuries ago: the Devil's Ring, the Devil's Finger, the Giants' Graves, and so on.

The different types of giant stone monuments have also received names drawn from the old Celtic language of Wales and Britanny. Monuments consisting of a single standing stone are called "menhirs," from the Breton words *men*, "stone," and *hir*, "long." Those consisting of several parallel stones on end with a roofing stone set like a tabletop across them are known as "dolmens," from *dol*, "table," and *men*, "stone." A circle of megaliths is a "cromlech," from *crom*, "circle," and *lech*, "place." The French word *alignement* is used to describe megaliths arranged in rows to form long processional avenues.

Archaeologists dislike these words. They find them too romantic, too deeply flavored by the magic of a dead language. Instead of speaking of menhirs and cromlechs and dolmens, they talk of "single standing stones" and "grouped standing stones" and "passage chambers." Grudgingly they will refer to a stone as a menhir, perhaps, in a moment of weakness, but the simple stone-roofed monuments called dolmens are

*158*   rarely spoken of that way by archaeologists, who regard them as early examples of a much more complex kind of structure. The dolmens and menhirs no longer interest them much anyway. Not even the cromlechs, the megalithic temples that are so fascinating to laymen, are at the center of archaeological attention. The archaeologists concentrate on the least conspicuous of the megalithic monuments—the underground chambered tombs. From these dark, somber burial places has come that part of the story of the megalithic religion that we have been permitted to learn.

The chamber tombs were constructed in various ways, depending on the location and the time when they were built. Some were cut into the rock of a cliff, but most were made of megalithic slabs of stone set on end and roofed by horizontal slabs. Often these stone tombs were covered with earth after they were completed, so that all that was visible was a low, sloping mound on which grass and shrubbery grew.

These mounds, which the English call "barrows," are found by the thousands all over western Europe. Farmers leveling their land frequently dug the barrows apart and discovered that they contained skeletons and ancient artifacts. The collectors of antiquities provided a ready market for the weapons, ornaments, and clay vessels that the barrows contained, and for hundreds of years the ransacking of the barrows went on with no pretense at scientific investigation. This was particularly true in England, where from the seventeenth century on it became a gentlemanly pursuit to open barrows and collect their contents. That this was grave robbing did not trouble anyone's conscience; what was far worse, the random looting of the barrows deprived later archae-

ologists of a chance to study their contents systematically.

However, there were so many barrows that not
even the Sunday pot hunters could demolish all of
them. With the rise of scientific archaeology in the
nineteenth century, they came at last under careful
observation. The megalithic tombs were recognized
as Stone Age monuments, and hundreds of them
were carefully excavated and studied. The basic
form, it was now realized, was a chambered barrow
containing several rooms, or a single room reached
by a long stone passageway. The "passage graves"
were the most elaborate kind, with lengthy galleries
of stones on edge roofed by other stones, a sort of
extended dolmen, leading to the chamber or chambers. Other barrows simply contained a square stone
vault, a kind of box of stone, which could be entered
only through the roof.

Obviously these were burial chambers. They contained human skeletons, often a great many of them,
along with objects that apparently had been placed
beside the dead as signs of honor or as things to use
in the next world. Pottery, weapons, flint blades and
scrapers, polished stone axes, and other "grave
goods" were found. The presence of charred animal
bones indicated that some sort of burnt-offering
sacrifice may have been part of the funeral ritual.

Though the dead were clearly buried with great
ceremony in the megalithic tombs, their remains did
not seem to be treated with much respect thereafter.
The chambers contained multiple burials, a dozen or
more skeletons in the same room, sometimes as many
as fifty or a hundred. Only one or two of these
skeletons were in good condition; the rest were
broken and crumpled, as though they had been
rudely pushed aside to make room for the newest

arrival in the tomb. One chamber only seven feet by five contained thirteen skeletons. The chambered tombs must have remained in use for centuries, the honored dead of one generation becoming the worthless clutter of the next.

The presence of stone axes and knives in the tombs told the nineteenth-century archaeologists that they were dealing with the work of prehistoric man. Passage-grave tombs were found in a wide arc from North Africa to Scandinavia, and though there were local differences in construction and contents, they all clearly belonged to a single culture. As the Danish archaeologist Conrad Englehardt wrote in 1870, "They are on the whole confined to the coastal stretches, to the lowlands and the river valleys. Considered as a whole, they are all of identical ground plan and mode of construction, and their monumental character appears to have originated in one and the same culture."

Along the southern curve of this arc, from North Africa up through Portugal, Spain, and southern France, the passage graves often proved to hold Bronze Age relics. The megalithic tombs of northern France, Great Britain, Ireland, and Scandinavia yielded few if any metal objects. Since the use of metal had come to Europe from the Mediterranean lands, spreading gradually northward, it seemed likely that the passage-grave idea had taken the same route, arising in Bronze Age territory and moving toward the countries of the north, which were still in the Stone Age.

The time of the Megalith Builders can be placed confidently in the late Neolithic. The presence of polished stone tools in the tombs testifies to that, as do the bones of domestic animals. The bronze objects that were found were of an early sort. As the dating system for prehistoric Europe was worked out, the passage-grave era was shown to have begun about five thousand years ago—roughly when the Lake Dwellers were driving their first piles into the mud —and to have reached its peak ten to fifteen centuries after that.

The story of the megalithic religion has occasionally been blurred by local patriotism. Scandinavia, for example, is rich with passage graves, and some Swedish and Danish archaeologists have devoted considerable effort to proving the theory that the megalith cult began there and spread *southward*. However, the opinion more widely held is that the great stone tombs of the northern countries represent an independent development that only coincidentally resembles the passage-grave tombs of the other lands. There is no reason why the idea of building tombs from huge slabs of stone could not have been invented simultaneously in two separate parts of the world. The Megalith Builder culture that covered most of Europe forty centuries ago appears to be unrelated to the culture that built the northern tombs.

The custom of burying the dead in chamber tombs can be traced to the eastern Mediterranean region. About fifty centuries ago, mass burials in stone tombs became customary among the people of the islands of Crete, Rhodes, and Cyprus. These islands had rich, sophisticated cultures then. They had already learned the use of metals and the mysteries of architecture. The islands had extensive merchant fleets, which visited every Mediterranean port. These island merchants grew wealthy by serving as middlemen between the older and even more advanced civilizations of the Near East and the backwoodsmen of Europe. Vessels from Cyprus and Crete plied the Mediterranean, calling at the ports of Syria and Asia Minor to pick up goods from Babylonia and

*162*  Egypt, and carrying this merchandise westward to the shores of Italy, France, and Spain, where eventually other traders brought it inland to northern Europe.

On these eastern Mediterranean islands the dead were buried in caves cut into the soft rock of the hillsides. Where no such rock-cut tombs could be constructed, the islanders built above-ground tombs from blocks of stone. These were generally family tombs, which remained in use for many generations. Their design varied from island to island.

Such burial customs seem to have been related to the worship of a mother goddess in the Near East. The mother goddess, under many names and in many guises, has long played a major role in man's religious thought. Pregnant women shown in the Aurignacian cave paintings may have been mother goddesses of twenty-five thousand years ago. Demeter of the Greeks, Ceres of the Romans, Isis of the later Egyptians, all were forms of the mother goddess. She survives in Christianity, some anthropologists maintain, in the form of the Virgin Mary. The mother goddess is the deity of the earth, of fertility, of birth, of the growth of crops. It is she who brings forth new life each year in the green miracle of springtime. Farmers everywhere have turned to her in prayer. The mother goddess of the Mediterranean islands is shown again and again in female statuettes that remind us of the Venuses of the Gravettian mammoth-hunters. Figurines and engravings found on the Mediterranean islands show her full body and her round, staring, all-seeing eyes. Some archaeologists speculate that the building of rock-cut or underground chambered tombs grew directly out of this cult of the mother goddess, for such a burial might symbolize the return of the body to Mother Earth at the end of its span of days.

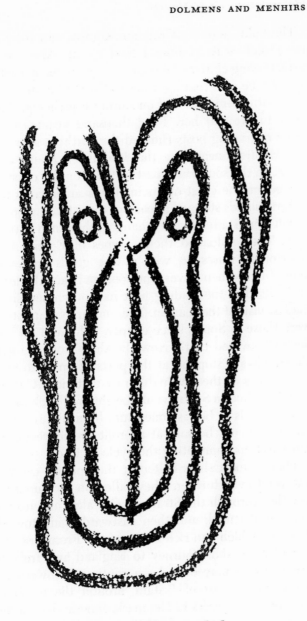

*Mother Goddess symbol.*

*164*     The bold sailors of Crete and Cyprus and Rhodes made their way westward through the Mediterranean, staying close to shore and calling at many ports. We may be sure that figurines of the mother goddess went with them, and that on stormy seas they paused often to pray to her. Four thousand years ago, a string of trading posts rimmed the northern shore of the Mediterranean, on the islands of Malta and Sicily, on the southeast coast of Italy, on the coast of France, on the coast of Spain. The seamen from the eastern islands stopped at each of these trading posts, which were staffed by merchants of their own nationality. They unloaded their cargoes of Egyptian or Babylonian wares, as well as the goods from the home islands themselves, and took on board the local products that the trading post had purchased since the last visit of the seamen. The most important stops were those in Spain, since copper, gold, and tin had been discovered there. Now the ships from the east almost always stopped at the ports of Spain to take on supplies of these valuable raw materials. Copper and tin mined in Spain would be shipped back to the home islands to be fashioned into bronze knives and axes that could be sold at a profit to the people of Europe, thus completing the cycle of trade.

Though most ships halted at the Spanish coast, a few went even further. They sailed on for hundreds of miles, through the Straits of Gibraltar and up the coast of Portugal, and then eastward again toward Brittany, which had rich mines of tin. From Brittany it was just a short journey to England and Ireland. Some vessels may even have continued onward up the western coast of Britain, around the north of Scotland, and across to Denmark, thousands of miles by sea from the warm isle of Crete.

Wherever they went, the bold captains of the Mediterranean paused to do business, and if possible to plant a colony that would serve as a trading post where later voyagers could call. And, wherever they went, these rovers of the sea carried their religion. When a man of Crete or Rhodes or Cyprus died in a cold foreign land, his shipmates built a stone tomb for him after their own fashion, and performed a service for him according to the rituals of the mother goddess. Those who remained behind as traders also served as missionaries, bringing the gospel of the passage-grave cult to the natives of Europe. And so the Mediterranean creed spread, westward and then northward along the coasts, carried by the seamen of the Bronze Age islands to the Stone Age folk with whom they traded.

This is the current archaeological interpretation of the evidence, at any rate. It may be as wrong as Ferdinand Keller's picture of Swiss villages on platforms over lakes, of course. The best we can say is that, as of now, we think the megalith idea came to Europe in this way. The archaeologists themselves disagree on the details. Some picture the builders of the megalithic tombs as, to quote the English archaeologist Glyn Daniel, "some sort of travelling undertakers persuading the natives to adopt a new style of tomb." Others see them as religious missionaries, others as colonists, others as roving prospectors for precious metal. Dr. Daniel, who has devoted much study to this problem, believes that "in the absence of written evidence we may go on arguing forever about the historical role of the Megalith Builders, and there may indeed be an element of truth in all the theories. Each writer must try to convey his own mixture of prospectors, undertakers, missionaries, colonists."

We have already seen that the whole Neolithic revolution was exported to Europe by the advanced civilizations of the Near East. As early as eight

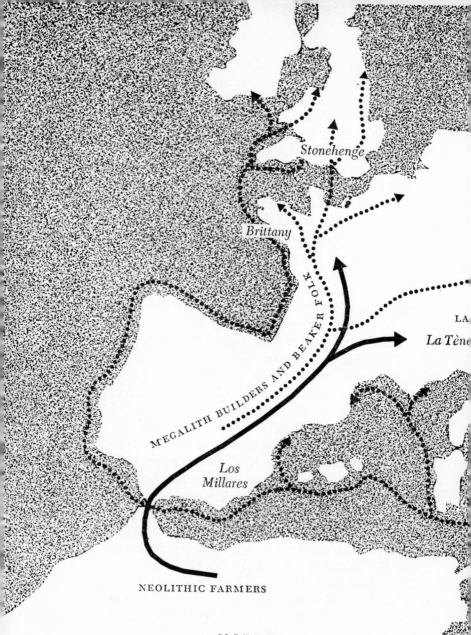

Stonehenge

*Brittany*

MEGALITH BUILDERS AND BEAKER FOLK

LA

*La Tène*

*Los Millares*

NEOLITHIC FARMERS

NORTH AFRICA

NEOLITHIC
SITES AND
MIGRATIONS

BATTLE-AXE PEOPLE

HEN
ENS

mber
oute

VELLERS

onica
lley

Halstatt

Nea
Nikomedeia

NEOLITHIC FARMERS

ASIA MINOR

Sicily

Mycenae

Rhodes

Sea
Trade
Routes

Crete

Jericho

EGYPT

thousand years ago, we know, farmers were crossing out of Asia Minor into Bulgaria and Greece and founding villages. This was the eastern Neolithic migration that thrust on and on through the valley of the Danube into central Europe until it reached Germany and Scandinavia. These people were forced to move along every few generations, because their primitive farming methods quickly exhausted the soil.

While this northwestward spread of Neolithic culture was going on, we have seen, another Neolithic prong was advancing in western Europe. It consisted of people also originally from Asia Minor and Syria who had moved westward along the Mediterranean, though perhaps their last stop before entering Europe was in North Africa. These were the people who brought Neolithic ways to Spain, France, Switzerland, and the British Isles. They were more advanced than the Mesolithic hunters they displaced; but they were backwoodsmen compared with the Bronze Age merchants whose vessels worked the Mediterranean ports.

The Stone Age farming folk of western Europe were the first converts to the megalithic religion that the merchant vessels brought. Since they were farmers, they responded warmly to the mother goddess cult, with its emphasis on fertility and the rebirth of springtime. They may even have brought a similar cult of their own with them on their migration. Whatever the reason, the Neolithic villagers took enthusiastically to the notion of burying their dead in huge stone-walled tombs. They became missionaries themselves, carrying the idea inland to places where the merchant seamen never reached. As the cult spread, it began to acquire local variations, though the basic megalithic idea was common to all areas. The earlier chambered tombs were round. This was the favorite pattern in southern Spain and Portugal, in Brittany, Wales, Ireland, and Scotland—all coastal regions that absorbed the teachings of the Mediterranean missionaries at first hand. The long, narrow, parallel-gallery style of passage grave developed inland, in northern Spain and northeast France, as the original idea became transformed by passing from village to village.

One of the most famous groups of round-chamber tombs is at Los Millares, on the southeast coast of Spain. Here, about 3400 B.C., colonists from the eastern Mediterranean built a trading post modeled after their native towns—a hilltop settlement fortified by a stone wall. The mother goddess was worshiped here, as is shown by the hundreds of stone plaques that represent her. And the cemetery at Los Millares contains seventy-five chambered tombs of large size. Their plan was simple: a circular stone chamber reached by a short passage, built above ground but covered by a mound of earth.

During the nine hundred years that Los Millares was occupied by the Megalith Builders, the style of tomb gradually changed, so that some passage graves in nearby districts came to have bottle-shaped or V-shaped chambers. The passage approaches became longer, and the tombs themselves now were placed underground, though still covered by circular mounds. About 2500 B.C. the settlement at Los Millares was destroyed, but by that time the passage-grave idea had taken firm hold and was moving inland through Spain.

Later, passage graves with rectangular chambers and long entrance passages became the preferred style. The most remarkable megalithic tomb of this kind is New Grange, in Ireland. New Grange is the largest of a number of passage graves in the valley of the Boyne River, about twenty-five miles north of

*170*   Dublin. It is a mound about two hundred and sixty-five feet in diameter and forty-four feet high, covering nearly an acre. Within is a passage sixty-two feet long and three feet wide, made of stones standing on edge. It leads to a cross-shaped central chamber—a main room and two side chapels—nearly twenty feet high. The stones comprising the walls of this vast chamber are richly ornamented with spirals, eyes, and other decorations thought to be connected with the cult of the mother goddess. Around the entire outside of the mound once stood a ring of similarly decorated megaliths, each as high as a man, but only a dozen of these remain; the rest were hauled away to be used as building stones by local farmers long before the importance of the mound was understood.

The eerie spirals, lozenges, zigzags, triangles, circles, and eye designs inscribed on the stones of New Grange merely hint at the nature of the rites once performed in the great tomb. Little in the way of grave goods has ever been found in it. The only passage grave of this period that has been studied with its original contents intact was excavated in 1961 at Tara, near Dublin. This is the so-called Mound of the Hostages, a small passage grave that turned out to hold chiefly the crumbled ash of cremated human bodies. Carbon-14 dating showed that the last cremation at that mound had taken place about four thousand years ago—five centuries after the destruction of Los Millares. Since the other European passage graves have contained whole skeletons, not ash, it appears that the rite of cremation was an Irish innovation that entered the religion fairly late.

Because they usually contain artifacts, the passage graves are considered the most important archaeological heritage from the Megalith Builders. The contents of a single grave can reveal more than an entire valley full of standing megalithic monuments. The menhirs and cromlechs, though, have a special fascination—particularly the most celebrated of all, Stonehenge. (Since it was not actually a product of the Megalith Builder culture, though it may have been inspired by earlier megalithic architecture, it is discussed in a later chapter.) The colossal stones standing upright in fields and valleys offer little clue to their purpose. They are not beautiful to behold. They are nothing more than gigantic slabs of rough stone, sometimes marked with the carved symbols of the megalithic religion: the eye, the axe, the sun, the outline of a ship. Sometimes we find a solitary menhir; sometimes they occur in great numbers, as in the *alignement* at Carnac in Brittany, where three thousand menhirs stand in eleven parallel lines.

We come to them. We stand before the silent stones. And we wonder what words the missionaries used, as they carried their cult of stone westward thousands of years ago. Not a word of their rituals survives, nor a syllable of their beliefs. But thousands of stone-walled tombs and titanic temples mutely tell us what power those rituals and beliefs once had over the minds and hearts of men.

# 11
# THE
# BEAKER
# FOLK

In 1849, a young intern at Guy's Hospital in Wiltshire, England, was browsing in the hospital museum when he came upon two skulls that had been dug up a generation earlier in a megalithic barrow. The intern's name was John Thurnam, and he went on to have a distinguished medical career. The impact of coming face to face, so to speak, with two men of the distant past was permanent, however. Dr. Thurnam became a diligent excavator of barrows himself, and one of Great Britain's outstanding authorities on the time of the Megalith Builders.

In the course of his investigations, he observed that the English barrows were of two kinds: long barrows and round barrows. The long barrows contained multiple burials of Stone Age date. Some of these were the megalithic graves discussed in the last chapter, and some the burial places of an earlier

174 Neolithic culture. The round barrows were quite different. In them Dr. Thurnam discovered objects of stone and bone, to be sure, but also objects of bronze, iron, glass, amber, pottery, and other substances. Clearly they were later than the long barrows of the megalithic people. There was also a notable difference between the skeletons found in the two types of barrows—a fact Dr. Thurnam, an expert on the structure of the brain, could not fail to notice. The long barrows held the skeletons of people with long, narrow skulls. The round barrows held the skeletons of people with round skulls.

"Long barrows, long skulls; round barrows, round skulls"—every student of British archaeology knows that catch phrase. It was evident that the round-skulled people of the round barrows were members of a wholly new group that had entered the British Isles well after the peak of the passage-grave movement. Almost always, their tombs contained pottery drinking cups of an unusual and attractive bell-shaped pattern. They became known as bell-beakers, and the round-skulled newcomers were dubbed the Beaker Folk. Dr. Thurnam described their beakers this way:

"They are usually tall vessels of seven or eight inches in height, thin and well-baked . . . the colouring varying from a light brown to a somewhat bright red. The general capacity is from two to three pints, though a few contain less than one, and others as much as four pints. The ornamentation is profuse; the surface, covered with markings incised or punctured, symmetrically arranged in horizontal bands, which, in the more ornate, alternate with squares, oblong or checker-shaped compartments, placed vertically or obliquely, and variously filled in."

These observations, published in 1869, established the Beaker Folk as one of the important cultures of

Bronze Age Britain. Bell-beakers were found in large numbers of barrows in southern England, not quite so often in northeastern England and eastern Scotland, and not at all (or so it was thought) in Ireland. The Beaker Folk did not begin to fit into the larger picture of European prehistory until 1912, though. In that year, a youthful Swedish archaeologist named Nils Aaberg, who had been going through excavation reports from many places, observed that bell-beakers identical to the British type had been uncovered in Brittany, Spain, southern France, Holland, Germany, and even deep in central Europe east of Austria. Some further research produced the information that bell-beakers could also be traced to Portugal, Poland, Sardinia, Sicily, and many other parts of Europe—including Ireland, where they had long eluded discovery. The handsome, distinctive beakers were all of the same style. The prehistorians now saw that the Beaker Folk must have been an aggressive, active, widely traveled breed.

The trademarks of the Beaker Folk were easy to recognize, once attention had been called to them. The round skulls and the elegant reddish-brown drinking vessels were almost always accompanied by other typical objects. One of the most common was a curved rectangular plate, about four inches long and an inch or two wide, made of stone or bone or occasionally baked clay. Such plates were usually found with holes pierced in each of the four corners, and at first they were thought to have had some ritual significance. Then a well-preserved example was found in England. It had a gold-headed stud in each corner hole, mounted on a bronze rivet to which a leather strap had once been attached. The plate rested on the wristbones of a skeleton, and beneath the wrist was a small metal buckle. The function of the oblong plates was now clear to anyone who had

176  ever practiced archery: they were wrist guards, designed to protect the wearer's left arm against the painful twang of the bowstring. (*Photograph, page 196.*)

The presence of finely chipped flint arrowheads in Beaker Folk burials is further proof of their pursuit of archery, while the bones of hawks found in some tombs testify that they were falconers as well. The tombs of many Beaker Folk men were also decked with weapons clearly intended to accompany warriors to their graves: magnificent battle-axes of bronze or polished stone, and bronze or flint daggers with broad, deadly looking blades. The evidence of the burials leads us to see these people as proud, swaggering, and warlike, placing great value on the qualities of strength and courage.

The frequency with which bronze weapons and tools were found in Beaker Folk graves means that, unlike the Megalith Builders who lived in western Europe before them, they were familiar with the use of metal. The Neolithic farmers who converted to the megalithic religion between five thousand and four thousand years ago were not able to manufacture their own metal implements, though they bought them eagerly from the Mediterranean missionary-merchants. But the Beaker Folk were Bronze Age people themselves. They were the first native Europeans to learn the metalworkers' art and turn it to their own profitable advantage.

During the 1920's, archaeologists in many parts of Europe sought to unravel the mystery of the Beaker Folk. It was clear that these round-headed voyagers had infiltrated much of Europe about four thousand years ago. Where had they come from? Where was the center of their culture? The clues emerged gradually—a trail of bell-beakers and wrist guards, leading southwestward across Europe, until by 1928 the answer was clear. The Beaker Folk had originated in Spain.

Spain had the rich mines of copper and tin that could spark the development of a Bronze Age culture. For centuries, the metal-using people of the eastern Mediterranean had maintained trading posts in Spain for the purpose of buying the valuable metals from the natives. At first, the ancestors of the Beaker Folk were glad to do business with the foreigners. They mined metals and brought their raw material to towns like Los Millares, where they exchanged it for the daggers and trinkets of the east. At that same time, no doubt, the merchants at the trading posts preached the megalithic religion to the Spanish miners.

The local people were alert and clever. They learned how to make use of their own ores, how to melt copper and tin and fuse them into bronze, how to cast and hammer the bronze into axe blades and daggers. A time came when they no longer cared to sell raw metal to the swarthy merchants from Crete and Cyprus. Perhaps these emerging Bronze Age people of Spain were the ones who sacked and destroyed the Megalith Builder city at Los Millares about 2500 B.C. In any case, they rejected the megalithic religion and set themselves up as merchants in their own right.

Out from Spain the Beaker Folk moved—tall, rugged, round-headed people of great strength and authority. They followed the routes blazed for them by the megalithic missionaries a thousand years before. To Brittany, to the shores of Scandinavia, to Italy, to Portugal, to the Netherlands—they sailed both east and north from Spain, bearing implements of bronze for sale.

They traveled in small groups, cautiously extend-

*178* ing their zone of influence decade after decade. First came an advance party to scout the territory, half a dozen men or so, well armed and ready to meet any show of force. They must have caused a ripple of excitement that preceded them by days as they journeyed. The Neolithic farmers, seeing a ship on the horizon, might think it was a craft of the Mediterranean traders who had been visiting them as long as anyone could remember. But then the Beaker Folk would step ashore, proud strangers in fine woven cloaks, carrying quivers of arrows on their backs and gleaming bronze daggers at their sides. They looked like warriors, but they had come to do business. They had splendid blades of good Spanish metal to barter for local products.

After the vanguard had made its safe landing, the permanent force of Beaker Folk colonists followed. They set up a trading post and settled down for a long stay. Keeping aloof from the peasants of the neighborhood, perhaps, they continued to speak their own language among themselves, and to worship their own gods. But they were always ready to do business, trading the bronze goods of Spain for whatever of value the natives could offer—furs, amber, semiprecious stones such as jadeite or jet. By 1900 B.C there were Beaker Folk settlements along the east and south coasts of England, and new landings were made every year. On the European mainland, too, the Spanish traders moved steadily inland, following the valleys of the great rivers, reaching into the Rhineland and toward the Danube.

All about them were farmers who practiced the megalithic religion. The Beaker Folk had their own ideas about the burial of the dead, and did not care to build passage graves where many bodies would be laid to rest. A man of the Beaker Folk wished to be buried alone. In some places, they took over existing megalithic tombs, cleaning them out and making them ready for a proper Beaker Folk funeral. Where no existing tombs were available, they dug new ones. A single body was buried in each, surrounded by the objects that had meant so much to the living man: his dagger, his bow and arrows and wrist guard, his finest cloak, his favorite hawk, which had hunted with him on days of recreation. Into the grave, too, went a few of the fine buff-hued beakers that the women of the trading post made with such skill. The grave was sealed, and a mound of earth was heaped up over it.

As the years passed, the Beaker Folk no longer came to seem so strange to the native people of western Europe. At first they had been occasional visitors, and then they had been the lordly proprietors of the trading post, but now they were simply part of the local scene. They had lost touch with their homeland and now spoke the local language, followed local ways, and married into the families of local chieftains. It was no longer necessary for caravans to bring bronze wares all the way from Spain to the remote outposts of the Beaker traders. Now forges existed at many places along the trade routes, and the copper and tin of England was being fashioned into sturdy bronze on the spot. Blending into the native populations, the Beaker Folk carried much of Europe with them into the Bronze Age. The secrets of their craftsmanship passed to the peasants of France and Britain and Germany. Those earlier traders, the Megalith Builders, had brought with them a religion; but the Beaker Folk had given the mastery of metal to their customers.

The Beaker Folk were the most diligent merchants who worked the trade routes of Europe four thousand years ago, but they were not the only ones. The prosperous people of the eastern Mediterranean were

*180*  still active. Their ships no longer went so often toward Spain and beyond, because the Beaker Folk had gained a firm hold on the markets of western Europe. But they had developed useful overland routes into the rapidly developing heart of the continent.

Crete remained the most important of the island kingdoms of the Mediterranean. Its great civilization had spread to the Greek mainland, and mighty cities like Mycenae and Tiryns had been founded. By 1750 B.C. these mainlanders had grown so important that they dominated Mediterranean shipping. Vessels of the Mycenaean civilization now were common sights in the ports of the Syrian coast, and as far west as Italy and Sicily.

The Mycenaeans did not neglect their backwoods cousins of northern Europe. From the far north came a commodity that the princes of Mycenae and Crete valued highly: amber. Amber, the fossilized resin of ancient evergreen trees, was coveted for its rich yellow color and glossy texture, which made it attractive for beads, pendants, and other ornaments. The chief source of amber was the shore of the Baltic Sea, where it could be dug from the sandy beaches, or even found washed up on land. To reach the coasts of Denmark and northern Germany by sea meant an endless voyage around half of Europe; the Mycenaeans found it much more practical to establish an overland amber route from Denmark to Italy.

A British archaeologist named J. M. de Navarro was able to map the amber route in 1925, basing his theories on the places where amber artifacts had been found. He showed the ancient route running from Denmark down the Elbe River into Germany, across the Alps, through the Adige Valley in Italy to the mouth of the River Po, where ships waited to carry the precious substance eastward to Mycenae and Crete. Many places along the amber route have provided recent archaeologists with an exciting view of the meeting of different cultures.

One of the most rewarding sites is Camonica Valley in the Italian Alps, a central point on the ancient route. Here, a thousand miles from Scandinavia and a thousand miles from Mycenae, the merchants of the Mediterranean mingled with the farmers of the north, and cunning artists recorded the interchange in a wondrous collection of rock-carved pictures.

Camonica Valley lies north of the city of Brescia. It is a fifty-mile-long gash in the high, snow-covered mountain wall known as the Alps, a natural pass through which the amber-laden caravans could travel with ease. Archaeologists knew that the valley had been conquered by the Romans in 16 B.C., and that it had probably been inhabited for a few centuries before the Romans came. But for a long time they had no knowledge of the valley's prehistoric importance.

The villagers of Camonica Valley knew that certain rocks in their neighborhood bore mysterious carvings, dimly visible beneath a crust of moss and soil. The images of men and beasts and chariots could be seen—possibly the work of evil spirits, the villagers thought. They had but one feeling about these "haunted" rocks: stay away!

In 1914, one of the carved rocks came to the attention of an Italian archaeologist. He examined it, published an article about it, and let the matter drop. Sixteen years later, two other archaeologists returned to the rock and studied it again. More engraved rocks were discovered soon after. By 1954, better than twenty were known in the valley, and there was talk of beginning an extensive archaeological survey.

Still, nothing had been done by 1956, when twenty-five-year-old Emmanuel Anati visited the valley.

The Italian-born Anati had settled in Palestine in 1945, had fought in the Israeli army during Israel's war of independence, and then had begun to study archaeology at the Hebrew University in Jerusalem. While taking part in an archaeological expedition to Israel's Negev Desert, Anati discovered, in 1953, thousands of prehistoric rock carvings. To learn more about such carvings, he toured the places in Europe where they could be found. He planned to spend a day at Camonica Valley.

Guided by a local carpenter who had made himself an expert on the Camonica carvings, Anati inspected the valley. "Of most of the rocks, only small patches showed above the earth," he wrote later. "The bulk of the rocks disappeared beneath the grass and moss. It seemed probable that the engravings continued underground, and this proved to be so when I scraped away the soil and grass around one of the rocks. The newly cleaned section showed other carvings. Continuing our search, we soon discovered, around the zones already prospected, more rocks unknown till then and entirely covered with all kinds of figures. Under the moss and growth of the slopes there existed an enormous prehistoric collection, an inestimable artistic treasure."

Anati stayed a week in the valley, not a day. Glowing with the wonder of what he had seen, he began organizing an expedition. With a few friends, he returned to clean and photograph the carvings, and he used the photographs to win the financial support of several Italian institutions. In 1958 Anati commenced real excavations. By 1961, he was able to report that "nearly six hundred engraved rocks are known to us, including over twenty thousand rock pictures spread over an area fifty miles long."

The carvings often were jumbled together in tangled confusion; when the prehistoric artists had run out of bare rock faces, they simply chiseled over the works of their predecessors. Patiently, Anati and his colleagues sorted out these thousands of carvings. They showed humans and animals, buildings, vehicles, plows, looms, weapons, tools, nets, traps, and other realistically depicted objects. There were carvings of isolated feet and hands, geometric designs, abstract figures, and elaborate mazes. Finally there were short inscriptions in alphabetic characters, marking the period when writing reached Camonica Valley.

It was easy to date the alphabetic inscriptions. They could have been carved no earlier than 500 B.C. The pictures of such weapons as the sword, the lance, and the javelin could also be assigned to relatively recent times, after 750 B.C. But Camonica Valley had already been inhabited for at least a thousand years at that time. Anati was able to show that the earliest carvings were of Neolithic date, going back nearly four thousand years.

The carvings of the Stone Age artists of the valley were religious in nature. They show complex mazes and patterns of lines, figures of people with arms uplifted in prayer, and the round disk that represented the sun. This means that the megalithic religion, which the Mediterranean people brought to the coastal areas of Europe, did not reach inland to Camonica Valley. Instead of the symbols of the mother-goddess cult, the rocks of the valley display the designs common to a rival religion that had many followers in Neolithic northern Europe: a cult of sun worship. The sun-worshippers apparently spread their cult from Scandinavia southward across Europe. It made no headway in the lowland regions where the megalith religion was established, but it found followers in the mountainous heart of Europe. Solar disks—often shown riding in chariots—were

*Camonica Valley rock carving. Central figure holds a solar disk.*

carved on rock walls wherever the sun cult reached.

About 1600 B.C., the valley dwellers entered the Bronze Age. Rich supplies of copper ore lay all about them, and now they learned how to make use of it. That means they had started to have contact with the metal-using cultures south of the Alps. Perhaps they had begun exporting their ores to the more advanced people in the south, and then had come to learn from them the arts of metallurgy.

Now Camonica Valley was linked to two very different cultural groups: the sun-worshipping Neolithic folk of the north, and the prosperous Bronze Age people to the south. The northerners had amber; the southerners wanted it. Camonica Valley became a way station for the amber trade, and strangers now were common sights there. The rock carvings of this period show daggers and chariots in the Mycenaean style, and the first pictures of plows. Bronze blades manufactured in the valley found their way to Mycenae, and at least one has been discovered there by archaeologists. Fair-haired men of Scandinavia came to Camonica bearing amber, which the middle-men of the valley bought and sold to the Mycenaean voyagers. Not only merchandise but ideas passed along the amber route, so that war chariots of Mycenaean fashion came to be carved on the rocks of Sweden.

The meeting of different cultures meant the inter-change of customs. Camonica Valley is important to us because its vivid rock carvings give us an insight into the flow of goods and thoughts that linked pre-historic Europe some thirty-five hundred years ago. Once we begin to see the men of the past as voyagers and merchants, rather than as barbaric savages, the gulf between history and prehistory dwindles to the vanishing point. As Emmanuel Anati puts it, "Stand-ing before the storied rocks to which the Camunians entrusted their heritage, we feel as though the wor-shippers, laborers, sorcerers, priests, chieftains, and warriors of this ancient people are speaking to us and telling us their tale. . . . A bond is created between them and us: before our eyes unfold two thousand years of life in that Alpine valley; and in the everyday problems of this people, in their beliefs, in their social relations we discern our own image."

At this busy time, Beaker Folk were penetrating Europe from their base in Spain, and Mycenaeans were entering the continent from the opposite end of the Mediterranean. A third inward movement was also going on, this one beginning in the far northeast, on the plains of Russia. It was not a movement of merchants, but rather a gradual invasion by nomadic charioteers.

186     Archaeologists call this folk the Battle-Axe People. They draw their name from the calling cards they left in archaeological sites sprawled across thousands of miles of Europe: superb battle-axes of polished stone. These extremely attractive weapons, six to eight inches long and often made of some ornamental stone that could take a bright gloss, first were discovered in large quantities in Scandinavia in the nineteenth century. Just as the Beaker Folk were at first thought to be a local British culture, the Battle-Axe People were originally considered to have arisen in Denmark and Sweden. Then, as the evidence came in from other lands, the true range of the culture became known. The Battle-Axe People could be traced eastward into Russia. Their starting point was near the Black Sea. Like an unstoppable tide, they had rolled across Europe until they reached the Atlantic.

By the standards of their time, they were backward, even primitive. They did not know how to use bronze. They were slightly acquainted with the use of copper, but relied on stone for their tools and weapons. They knew little or nothing about agriculture. In many ways they were throwbacks to the old Mesolithic hunters who had occupied Europe before the coming of the Neolithic farmers.

But they had one skill that the early hunters had lacked: they knew how to tame animals. On that the entire Battle-Axe culture rested. They had collected great herds of cattle, which supplied them with milk and meat. And they had tamed the horse and harnessed him to a chariot of war. Aboard those triumphant chariots the Battle-Axe People came riding westward on a campaign of conquest.

It is easy enough to picture their arrival in Europe as a time of bloody butchery—a sudden and violent invasion, a spilling forth of wild nomads onto settled civilized towns. There is no archaeological evidence to support this picture, though, no bone heaps and piles of skulls telling grim tales of ancient massacres. It seems more likely that the advance of the Battle-Axe People was slow and determined. They were tough and forceful. They had come into Europe not out of the mere love of slaughter, however, but rather in search of new lands where they could graze their herds. As each grassland region in turn was exhausted, they moved westward toward the next, driving their flocks before them. Inevitably, they came into contact with the farmers of eastern and central Europe. To these farmers, it must have seemed wisest not to resist. They permitted some of their fields to become pastures for the invaders, and probably with resignation accepted the Battle-Axe People as their masters.

In this way, the herdsmen of Russia found their way to the Danube and to the Rhine, and onward toward Scandinavia, carving out grazing territories for themselves as they moved. They had much to learn from the people they invaded, but they had much to teach as well. Prehistorians believe that the Battle-Axe People introduced into Europe the ancestor of most of the languages of today. It is known that virtually all European languages, as well as Persian and many languages of India, belong to a common family of tongues, the Indo-European group. English, French, German, Swedish, Polish, Latin, Greek, Hindustani—all are based on one source. We see this when we look at the key words of a language, those that must have developed at the outset. Compare the English word "father" to its equivalents in other languages: *Vater* in German, *padre* in Spanish, *pater* in Latin, *pitar* in the old Indian language known as Sanskrit. The family relationship is obvious. Modern linguistic authorities,

searching for the roots of language the way archaeologists dig for the fragments of lost cultures, believe that the charioteers of the east brought the
ancestral language to Europe about four thousand
years ago.

They also brought their religion, the sun cult that
took hold so firmly in Scandinavia. As we have noted,
an important emblem of that cult was the solar disk
atop a wheeled chariot—and the chariot was a spe-
cialty of the Battle-Axe People. They taught their
skills as horsemen and cattle herders to the peasants
of Europe, even while they were learning from them
the techniques of agriculture. East of the Rhine, a
new kind of society took shape, with an aristocracy
of Battle-Axe People ruling over a peasantry of the
old Neolithic farming stock. The masters rode in
chariots, carried polished battle-axes and long daggers, and worshipped the sun. The conquered farmers
went on foot, used flint axes and knives, and practiced their old religion, of which we know nothing.
Gradually the language of the conquerors, and the
sun cult as well, filtered down to the conquered ones.

West of the Rhine a different sort of community
existed. It was made up of the western Neolithic
peoples who had begun migrating to Europe long
before. They had adopted the megalithic religion
about 3000 B.C., and a thousand years later they had
begun to learn metallurgy from the Beaker Folk.
They knew of the steady westward advance of the
Battle-Axe People, and no doubt wondered uneasily
when it would be their turn to fall.

The Beaker Folk themselves had no fears of the
chariot riders from the east. To them, the Battle-Axe
People simply represented a new market. Beaker
Folk merchants in the trading posts along the Danube and the Rhine greeted the Battle-Axe People in
a friendly way and immediately began doing busi-

ness with them. The Beaker Folk had something to offer that the Battle-Axe People very much desired: fine axes and daggers of bronze.

We can see the crisscrossing lines of commerce taking shape: Beaker Folk in the west, Battle-Axe People in the east, Mycenaean and other Mediterranean civilizations in the south, moving to and fro through a Europe still populated by the Stone Age farmers of the megalithic religion and even by scattered remnants of the ancient Mesolithic hunting and fishing tribes. Camonica Valley stood at the crossroads, its carved rocks revealing the sun disk of the Battle-Axe People and the bronze daggers of Mycenae. Many cultures met there.

Each had something to offer to the new European pattern of life now taking shape. From all sides, streams of culture were flowing into central Europe. The heartland of the continent became a crucible in which the blending took place.

Out of this union of cultures came a mingled strain. Beaker Folk and Battle-Axe People and Megalith Builders met and joined. The Megalith Builders contributed their skills as farmers and sailors; the Beaker Folk offered their craftsmanship in metals; the Battle-Axe People provided a knowledge of cattle herding and horsemanship, as well as their sun religion and their language. Only the eastern Mediterranean peoples stood apart from this mingling process, for they were more advanced than any of the others, and haughty about it.

For about five hundred years central Europe churned this way, before the new culture finally emerged from the parent strains. While the mixing was going on, the westward migrations still continued. The faces of men turned toward the land of the sunset, toward the great ocean, toward the end of the world—toward Britain.

# 12
# STONEHENGE

"Westward the course of empire takes its way," George Berkeley wrote in 1735. He was speaking of the opening of the New World, the great westward drive that had carried European civilization into two new continents.

But that westward surge of civilization had been going on for thousands of years. The prevailing currents of ideas had almost always traveled from west to east and from south to north. Westward out of Asia Minor and the Near East had come the Aurignacians, spreading along the heart of Europe until they reached France and Spain. After the breakup of the great Ice Age cultures, the Mesolithic hunting and fishing techniques had followed the same route. Westward had swept one cultural phase after another, pumped outward from the source of knowledge in the east—the Neolithic revolution, the

*192*  religion of the Megalith Builders, the Bronze Age. Each new idea had passed across Europe until it reached the sea. That prevailing tide of culture led inevitably to the northwest, to the islands that looked out on the endless sea. Britain was the last stop for the wave of change.

In the Upper Paleolithic, when cave men flourished in France and Spain, Britain lay uninhabited beneath a sheet of ice. When the great thaw came, Maglemosean hunters made their way by boat to Britain, founding such settlements as Star Carr. For the next six thousand years these people had the British Isles to themselves. Undisturbed in their island homes, they lived the simple life of hunters, roving from place to place, feeding on wild game and wild plants. They grew no crops, tamed no herds, and made their tools by chipping flint, as their ancestors had done since the dawn of time.

Meanwhile great cultural upheavals were going on in Europe. The double columns of Neolithic farmers were entering the continent, one group by way of Bulgaria and Greece, the other from North Africa via Spain and France. These people were taking hold and building their villages everywhere. Then, about 3000 B.C., the Megalith Builders began to preach their creed to the farmers, and to win converts. Still Britain remained a land of roving hunters.

It is just a short sea voyage from Brittany in France to the southern coast of England. About 2500 B.C., possibly a century or two earlier, colonists from Brittany began to cross over onto the beaches of Wessex. These people were farmers whose way of life was much like that of the Lake Dwellers of Switzerland, their contemporaries. They lived in log cabins, raised wheat and other grains, and herded cattle.

*Alignment of menhirs at Carnac, France.*

*Dolmen near Carnac, France.*

*Interior of passage grave*
*at West Kennet, England.*

*Interior of passage grave*
*at West Kenett, England.*

Bell beaker, points and
wrist guard from a grave at
Dorchester, England.

Bronze sun chariot,
Danish National Museum.

*Stonehenge,*
*England. Aerial view.*

*Stonehenge,
detail of capstone construction.*
( OPPOSITE PAGE. )

*Stonehenge,
detail of trilithons.*

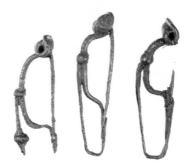

*Early metal objects
from Halstatt and La Tène:
shears and pins.*

*The face of Tollund Man,
Silkeborg, Denmark.*

Archaeologists call this first Neolithic culture of Britain the Windmill Hill People. They are named for a hilltop settlement they built near the present town of Avebury. Although they were able to produce their own food, the Windmill Hill People were cautious about venturing too deep into the British forests. Warily, they remained close to the sea, planting their crops on the chalky, lightly wooded uplands near the southern coast. They did not come into conflict with the hunting folk of the forests.

The Windmill Hill People left signs of their presence in the southern fringe of England that they occupied. They built large circular embankments of earth, which probably were cattle corrals for the autumn roundup of stock. They buried their dead under long mounds of chalk rubble. Some of the Windmill Hill barrows were hundreds of feet long and ten feet or more in height, and they contained several dozen bodies. These barrows differed from the passage graves of the megalithic sort, because the mounds did not contain stone-walled burial chambers at their centers. Hundreds of the long barrows remain in the part of England called Wiltshire.

A time came when the Windmill Hill People finally had to move northward. Their slash-and-burn method of clearing the forest for agriculture was successful for only a short time in one place; the soil quickly became exhausted and had to be left fallow for ten to twenty years. Clearing the forest as they went, the Windmill Hill farmers advanced up the eastern coast of England toward Yorkshire and Lincolnshire. They still left the heart of the country to the native hunting folk.

The western coast of England was also being colonized now. The ships of the Megalith Builders were starting to arrive. From about 2200 B.C. on, the missionaries of the new creed landed and settled. They were not the original eastern Mediterranean merchants who had first spread the religion eight centuries earlier, but rather converts of the western Neolithic stock, quite similar in culture to the Windmill Hill People. They cleared the forest, planted their crops, set their herds grazing. And they built their stone passage graves.

Living between these two Neolithic farming cultures, the forest hunters picked up some of their ways. They did not care to become farmers themselves, but they learned such useful things as how to make pottery and how to raise herds of cattle. These earliest Britons adopted a gypsylike life, roaming freely with their small flocks, hunting in the forests, fishing in the streams and on the shore. They became tradesmen of a sort, too, manufacturing flint and granite axes and peddling them to the farming towns in return for grain. Regular trade routes developed, as the axe traders made the rounds of the coastal settlements.

As they traveled, they learned a good deal about the religion of the farmers. The Megalith Builders must have explained to them the virtues of burying the dead in passage graves, while the Windmill Hill People no doubt sang the praises of their own form of worship, whose nature is unknown to us today. The axe traders listened; but, like the self-reliant wanderers that they were, they continued to follow a purely native kind of religion.

We think it was a sun-god cult, but that is only a guess. What we do know is that its rites were carried on in large open-air temples, circular or horseshoe shaped, ringed with wooden posts. The ruins of these structures are found in many parts of England. They all follow the same general plan: an enclosing bank of heaped-up earth on the outside, a ditch just within, and pits where free-standing posts once were mounted.

One of these open-air temples was built about 1900 B.C. in the middle of Salisbury Plain, some seventy miles west of London. Here, within an earthwork circle, wooden pillars were placed, and here the nomadic axe traders of England came to honor their gods. Scarcely a trace of that ring of wooden pillars remains. Instead, the stone columns of a later temple occupy the holy site. We call that temple Stonehenge. It is the best known prehistoric monument in Europe. (*Photographs, pages 197–199.*)

Stonehenge is megalithic in form—that is, it is made of giant stone slabs—but its construction does not seem to have been the work of the passage-grave people we call the Megalith Builders. Of all the many European cultures of the era, they alone do not seem to have had a hand in the building and rebuilding of the temple. The Stonehenge that exists today carries the imprint of the other waves of culture that swept across Europe toward England thirty to forty centuries ago.

Stand on windswept Salisbury Plain and study the Stonehenge of today, the battered ruin that time has left us. Wind and storm have overturned many of its towering slabs; misguided men have carried fragments away as souvenirs. Yet what remains is unforgettable. Start from Salisbury, eight miles away, the medieval cathedral town whose lovely streets are choked with modern traffic, and drive north eight miles or so, past the town of Amesbury. Come up over a rise in the road, and look down and to your left, and there is Stonehenge, gray against the green of the plain, seeming at this distance like the spiky skeleton of some extinct monster.

It costs a shilling or two to enter the monument. You pass a gate where tickets are sold, and walk a few hundred feet, and suddenly you stand within the Bronze Age temple itself. A rolling plain surrounds you, with low hills in the west. The horizon seems far away and the sky, glimpsed between the stones of Stonehenge, may look dark and menacing.

The pattern of Stonehenge is complex. There is an outer circle of gigantic stone blocks, cut from sarsen, a kind of sandstone. Some of the sarsens are capped by horizontal slabs. Once there was a continuous ring about a hundred feet in diameter, made up of thirty sarsen uprights weighing twenty-five tons apiece, capped by thirty seven-ton lintels, or horizontal slabs. Most of these have fallen.

Within the outer sarsen circle is a ring of smaller stones—still of great size themselves—known as the bluestones, from their color. Only a few bluestones are still in place from what was once a circle of sixty. They enclose a horseshoe-shaped grouping of sarsens even larger than the stones of the outer circle. These are the five trilithons, or "three-stones," so called because each is an arrangement of two uprights and a lintel. The huge uprights of the trilithons weigh as much as forty-five tons apiece.

And within the horseshoe of trilithons is what remains of a bluestone horseshoe that once numbered nineteen stones. At the center of this group lies a sixteen-foot-long block of sandstone that has become known as the Altar Stone. It formerly stood upright, but in A.D. 1620 the great central trilithon fell across it and buried it in the ground.

Several other features can be seen outside the stone temple itself. A ring of fifty-six pits, marked by chalky spots in the grass, encircles the entire monument. This in turn is ringed by a low embankment and a ditch, forming the outer borders of the sacred area. The ditch and embankment are broken on the northeast side by an entrance gap, and beside the entrance lies a large fallen stone that has received the romantic but probably inaccurate name of the

Heelstone

28 29 30 1 2 3 4 5
27 46 47 48 49 31 150 32
26 45 60 72 61 51 33 6
25 44 71 52 7
24 59 62 8
23 43 63 34 9
22 128 70 Altar Stone 64 53 35
21 58 69 65 54 10
57 68 67 66 36 11
20 56 55 37
19 41 39 38 12
18 40 13
17 16 15 14

■ Standing    ▨ Fallen    ○ Missing    ⊏⊐ Lintels

1-30    SARSEN CIRCLE
31-49    BLUESTONE CIRCLE
51-60    TRILITHONS
61-72    BLUESTONE HORSESHOE

Ditch and embankment, pits, Slaughter Stone and Heel Stone
may be seen in the aerial photograph, page 197.

*Plan of Stonehenge.*

206 Slaughter Stone. Many yards away, separate from everything else, stands a rough, gnarled-looking stone called the Heel Stone or the Devil's Heel.

That is Stonehenge: a hundred or so colossal stones, the smallest of them taller than a man, the biggest of awesome size. Even in its present shattered state, it inspires awe. R. J. C. Atkinson, the British archaeologist who has led the recent investigations of the monument, has written, "The huge mass of the stones, their upward taper, and the uncompromising four-squareness of the lintels which they support, together give an impression of forceful upward growth combined with an immense solidity and security. There is no top-heaviness, no feeling of impending ruin." Of the stones themselves, Atkinson writes, "no words of mine can properly describe the subtle varieties of texture and color, or the uncountable effects of shifting light and shade. From a distance, they have a silvery grey color in sunlight, which lightens to an almost metallic bluish-white against a background of storm clouds. . . . When the ground is covered in snow in midwinter, with a dull leaden sky threatening further falls, they seem nearly black; and at sunset in midsummer their surfaces glow, as if from within, with a soft warm pinkish-orange light."

Stonehenge has occupied the attention of the British for centuries. It first appears by name in English literature in a chronicle written about A.D. 1130, which called it one of the four wonders of Britain. Another historian, a few years later, suggested that the monument was the work of the magician Merlin. In 1620, the scholarly King James I commissioned the royal architect, Inigo Jones, to study Stonehenge in detail. Jones visited and sketched it, only a few months before the biggest of the trilithons went crashing down. It was his opinion that Stonehenge was the ruins of a Roman temple.

Inigo Jones' son-in-law John Webb published a book in 1655 setting forth Jones' view. It drew a hot rejoinder from another man who believed that the Danes had built Stonehenge after their conquest of England about the year 1000. Still another suggestion, and this a popular one, came from the antiquarian John Aubrey. Aubrey declared that Stonehenge, and several lesser stone circles nearby, had been temples of the Druids, that mysterious priesthood of early Britain.

No one knew much about the Druids, except that they were mentioned by certain Greek and Roman historians between 200 B.C. and A.D. 100. Those accounts called them the priests and judges of the tribesmen of western Europe, and dwelt in some detail on their bizarre and barbaric rituals. The idea of Stonehenge as a Druid temple caught the British imagination, and to this day many people believe—wrongly—that they were responsible. Actually, Stonehenge had been more than a thousand years old before the first Druid rites were performed, and may even have already been in ruins.

During the eighteenth and nineteenth centuries Stonehenge was constantly under study. It was measured, drawn, even partially excavated by men of archaeological bent, who were eager to discover the monument's Druid secrets. Tourists from London regularly made the long stagecoach trip to see the famed ruin, and a special hammer was kept in an Amesbury hotel to be rented to those who wished to knock off chunks of Stonehenge as keepsakes. The collapse of another trilithon during a winter storm in 1797 further disfigured the monument.

The archaeological discoveries in Europe during the nineteenth century helped to destroy the Druid theory and reveal the true antiquity of Stonehenge.

*208*   It became clear that the stone temple was much older than Druid times—that it went back to the early Bronze Age or even the Stone Age. In 1880 an archaeologist named William Matthew Flinders Petrie, who was later to become one of the great men of Egyptology, carried out the first careful modern study of Stonehenge. Twenty years later, an even more detailed examination by Professor William Gowland demonstrated the great age of the ruin.

Gowland had been asked by the British government to straighten and support an upright of one of the great trilithons, which had been leaning precariously for many years and now threatened to collapse. In the course of this assignment, he excavated at the base of the trilithon until he reached the foundation level. Below such things as Roman coins of the first century after Christ, Gowland found flint and sandstone axes and hammers that had been used in the construction of the trilithon. He suggested that Stonehenge had been built about 1800 B.C., at a time when metal tools were just coming into use but stone ones were still generally favored. He based this guess on the presence of a tiny green stain found on a chip of rock near the sandstone hammers. The stain was copper oxide, and told him that tools of copper or bronze had been used at least to some small extent in shaping the stones of Stonehenge.

While Professor Gowland was arriving at a date for Stonehenge through an examination of the buried evidence, an astronomer and mathematician named Sir Norman Lockyer was arriving at the same age for Stonehenge through an entirely different method. Those who fancied the Druid origin of Stonehenge had long maintained that the stones had been arranged in a particular relation to the sun or the stars, for some deep mystic significance in the ancient rites.

The astrologically inclined had noticed that a line drawn from the Heel Stone to the Altar Stone would pass through the center of the horseshoe-shaped groups of trilithons and bluestones in the middle of the entire construction. This line seemed clearly to mark the main axis of Stonehenge. Furthermore, it was seen that on Midsummer Day, June 21, an observer standing by the Altar Stone at dawn would see the sun rise practically over the Heel Stone.

From this it was concluded that Stonehenge had deliberately been constructed so that the sun would rise over the Heel Stone on June 21, the magical day that marks the beginning of summer. If the builders of Stonehenge were sun-worshippers, that day would have great importance for them, since it is the longest day of the year.

But the motions of the earth as it moves around its own axis change its position relative to the sun very slightly from year to year. In 1901, Sir Norman Lockyer noted, the sun no longer rose exactly over the Heel Stone. Carefully he computed the date in the past when the positioning of earth and sun had been such that the dawn of June 21 would put the sun in the proper place above the Heel Stone. He arrived at a date of 1840 B.C., give or take two hundred years, for the construction of Stonehenge.

Archaeologists today tend to smile at Sir Norman's calculations. They were made with the most precise astronomical equipment available, and so are far more accurate than any that the ancient architects could have made. Besides, some of Sir Norman's assumptions about where the Stonehenge builders figured their sunrise-point from do not necessarily coincide with the truth. Therefore his figures no longer are regarded as reliable. Ironically, they seem to be correct nevertheless. A carbon-14 date on a charcoal sample from one of the pits of Stonehenge

*210*  places the original date of construction as 1848 B.C. ±225 years. Using the wrong assumptions, Sir Norman seems to have landed at the right date!

Many archaeologists have worked at Stonehenge in the present century. A number of leaning stones were restored to a vertical position after the First World War under the direction of the archaeologist William Hawley, who also took the opportunity to excavate more than half the total area of the monument down to bedrock. Hawley's excavations answered many questions about the construction of Stonehenge, but later archaeologists do not look kindly on his methods, which often were destructive and clumsy. In 1950, fresh excavations were begun under the leadership of R. J. C. Atkinson, Stuart Piggott, and Dr. J. F. S. Stone, who interpreted their findings in the light of the many new discoveries in European archaeology. In the summer of 1958, more work was done in the course of re-erecting the trilithon that had collapsed in 1797. By now, most of Stonehenge has been dug up, and a fairly detailed picture of its history has been constructed.

The work of Stuart Piggott has shown that the original temple on the site was a wooden one built by the wandering axe traders, the original Britons, about 1900 B.C. This was the time at which the Beaker Folk of Spain were landing on the southern shore of England and founding their trading posts.

The coming of the Beaker Folk spelled bad news for the axe traders. The stone tools they had for sale could not begin to compete with the efficient bronze implements marketed by the newcomers from Spain. The axe traders began to fade away into the forests once again.

For two hundred years, the Beaker Folk had a clear field for commerce. Then competitors began to

arrive from Holland and the Rhineland. These were
Beaker Folk too, but they were the ones who had
mingled with the Battle-Axe People of central
Europe. Their beakers were of a slightly different
design. And they had adopted the sun-worship religion of the Battle-Axe People. These mixed Beaker-
Battle-Axe settlers quickly established themselves as
the dominant figures of British life. They built villages in south and central England and as far north
as Scotland. They also began to erect stone temples.

The site on Salisbury Plain attracted them. Probably the axe traders had abandoned it, and the Windmill Hill People, who were vanishing from the scene,
did not use it. Nothing was there except the circular
embankment and the ditch within it, the Heel Stone,
and the fifty-six pits that today are called the Aubrey
Holes. Possibly there was also a wooden arch or
gateway near the Heel Stone, and a ring of crum-
bling wooden uprights in the center of the area.

The Beaker-Battle-Axe People brought stone from
the west for their temple. They had often journeyed
westward to Ireland, a chief source of supply for the
copper they needed, and their route took them along
the south coast of Wales. There they noticed the
dark, attractive stone of the Prescelly Mountains, and
decided to use it for their temple. They carved some
eighty bluestones from the Welsh hills and trans-
ported them to Salisbury Plain. Since these stones
weighed up to four tons apiece, they were shipped
by water most of the way. Loaded on rafts or boats,
the stone blocks traveled 240 miles by sea and river
and were dragged overland the last few miles.

The builders arranged the bluestones in a double
circle at the center of the site. They left an entrance
on the northeast side, and dug a large pit on the
opposite side. A line drawn from the pit to the en-

trance and on through the Heel Stone would have pointed toward the rising sun on Midsummer Day.

This temple, recent work has shown, was never finished. The circle of bluestones was left incomplete, and two stones intended to mark the entrance were not put in place, though holes for them had been partially dug. Why this is so, we have no idea. But perhaps it has something to do with the complicated political upheavals that were taking place in Britain about 1600 B.C. All the cultural streams of Europe had now reached the British Isles, and the mixing process was at work. The Mesolithic axe traders, the Neolithic Windmill Hill and megalithic farmers, the pure Beaker Folk from Spain, the mixed Beaker and Battle-Axe People from Holland and the Rhineland, were all melding into a new culture. Archaeologists call it the Wessex culture. Taking form about 1500 B.C., it embraced the traits of all its predecessors.

It was a powerful, wealthy Bronze Age culture that enjoyed profitable contact with western Europe. The copper mines of Ireland and the tin mines of Cornwall were in full production, and raw materials flowed eastward in return for the goods of other lands. Scandinavian amber is common in the high, round burial barrows of the Wessex chieftains. So are gold ornaments that came from Crete and Mycenae. Even beads from far-off Egypt found their way to the fair women of Wessex. Britain was no longer the unknown end of the world; now it was a bustling, thriving commercial center where sun-darkened men of Crete could rub shoulders in the market place with Spanish merchants and with the proud horsemen of the Battle-Axe People.

Quite naturally, this complex, prosperous new British culture celebrated its grandeur by building temples. The Wessex people turned to Stonehenge, where the unfinished double circle of bluestones stood, and pulled it down. Leaving the discarded stones to one side, they brought more than eighty immense blocks of sarsen stone from the Marlborough Downs, twenty miles away. Since some of these great blocks weighed forty tons or more, and no convenient water route was available, hauling them must have been a man-killing task. Prehistorians think that the sarsens were mounted on rough sledges running on rollers, and dragged by men holding leather or cow-hair ropes. The project may have kept a thousand men busy for several years.

Once the huge sandstone blocks reached Stonehenge, they were used to construct the outer circle and inner horseshoe of linteled trilithons. The uprights were raised by digging foundation pits, sloping on one side and vertical on the other. Each upright was eased on rollers down the sloping side of the pit and propped up by logs. Men with levers then lifted the giant stone a few inches to permit another bit of timber to be slipped into place against the leaning block. Gradually it rose toward a vertical position and was pulled into final place by gangs of men hauling on ropes. Lastly, the foundation pits were filled and rammed tight. Into the pits went any material that happened to be on hand, including—as Professor Gowland showed in 1901—even the stone hammers and axes that had been used to shape and dress the surfaces of the blocks.

Placing the lintels or capstones was even more taxing. The workmen maneuvered each lintel into position on the ground in front of the pair of uprights on which it was going to rest. They raised it with levers and slipped timbers beneath it, first on one side and then on the other, so that the stone

*214*  slowly rose, still horizontal, on a crib of wood. When it was level with the tops of the uprights, twenty feet or more above the ground, it could be levered into place above them. The lintels were not simply balanced on the uprights; deep sockets were carved in them, into which were fitted projections that had been left on the tops of the uprights, locking the lintels to their supports.

When the job was finished, a magnificent circle of joined trilithons surrounded the inner horseshoe of even larger ones. The axis of this monument, like that of the bluestone circle it had replaced, pointed toward the midsummer sunrise. This, too, was a temple of the sun, where we can imagine that hushed worshipers gathered to greet the dawn on Midsummer Day.

There was nothing to equal Stonehenge anywhere in western Europe. The big slabs of stones had been squared and dressed with care and precision, and they had been arranged in a perfect circle that delighted the eye. The quality of the masonry and the high level of architectural accomplishment could be matched only in the eastern Mediterranean, where fine temples and palaces had been constructed for centuries.

Archaeologists had long suspected that the Wessex people hired architects and foremen from Mycenae or Crete to help them design the remodeled Stonehenge. The kinship of style suggested that members of the older civilization must have had a part in the work. This remained only a guess, though, until a day in the summer of 1953, when the setting sun cast its beams on one of the upright stones, illuminating the weathered surface and highlighting certain features not easily visible at other hours. The archaeologist R. J. C. Atkinson, glancing at the stone in this unfamiliar light, was startled to discover the unmistakable outline of a hilted dagger, point downward, and four axe heads, cutting-edge upward, carved just above eye level. Many other carvings of axe heads became known shortly afterward. What astonished Atkinson at first was that these carvings had gone unnoticed for so long. As he wrote, "Few people who have seen the Stonehenge dagger will deny that, once one knows where to look, it is perfectly obvious; indeed when the sun is shining across the face of the stone, it can be seen from the gate of the Stonehenge enclosure, over 100 yards away. Yet during the past three centuries hundreds of thousands of visitors must have looked at the dagger (to say nothing of the other carvings) without actually *seeing* it."

More surprising than the mere presence of the dagger was its unusual shape. The many axe heads were accurate copies of a type of bronze axe manufactured in Bronze Age Britain and exported to Europe. But the dagger, a foot long with a tapering blade and a large hilt, was of a Mycenaean type. Even the cautious archaeologists doubted that a native British workman would have carved the outline of a foreign dagger on the side of a Stonehenge upright. They see that long-unnoticed carving as convincing evidence that architects from the eastern Mediterranean were involved in the work.

Soon after the sarsen trilithons were erected, the discarded bluestones of the earlier temple were put to use. About twenty of them were chosen, squared and dressed, and mounted in an oval setting within the horseshoe of big trilithons. Some of these were made into miniature trilithons themselves. The builders apparently planned to use the remaining sixty bluestones this way, and dug holes to receive them. Then they abandoned the entire project. Per-

216    haps a change of architects occurred, or possibly some unlucky omen was detected by the priests. In any event, the bluestone oval was taken down.

The uprights of the small trilithons were rearranged to form the inner bluestone horseshoe of today's Stonehenge. Two of the bluestone lintels were set up as pillars flanking this group, but they have since fallen over. The rest of the bluestones, sixty in all, were set close together in a ring just within the outer circle of sarsen trilithons. Few of these remain. One big bluestone, which we call the Altar Stone, was placed before the central sarsen trilithon, and now is pinned under its fallen stones.

This was the final form of Stonehenge, reached about 1400 B.C. How long after that it remained in use, we do not know. The great Wessex culture that had built it came to an end, and Britain slipped back toward Stone Age simplicity. The stone temple on the broad plain was allowed to sink into decay. Its colossal trilithons toppled, and its lesser stones were carried off. Today only a few of the lintels are still in place, and it is not easy to conjure from the scattered slabs of stone a picture of what Stonehenge must have looked like when it was complete.

Yet even as it appears today, it stirs a sensation of wonder. All the many streams of the European past converge on the plain where Stonehenge stands. The early hunting folk had their temple here; the Beaker-Battle-Axe People replaced it with a finer one, perhaps drafting the Neolithic farmers to do the labor; then the rich Wessex culture remodeled the temple, possibly with the aid or supervision of architects of Mycenae, where the heroic King Agamemnon was born. Prehistoric sunlight splashed against these stones, and priests of an unknown rite performed their ceremonies of worship. No one can easily resist the power of Stonehenge. As an English antiquary,

William Cunnington, wrote nearly two centuries ago,
"Even the most indifferent passenger over the plain
must be attracted by the solitary and magnificent
appearance of these ruins; and all with one accord
will exclaim, 'HOW GRAND! HOW WONDER-
FUL! HOW INCOMPREHENSIBLE!' "

# 13
# THE FACE
# OF
# PREHISTORIC
# MAN

The doom of Stonehenge is shrouded in the mists of prehistory; but the dawn of the historic era is near. True, Europe in 1000 B.C. still lags behind other parts of the world in such matters as literacy and architecture. Egypt and Babylonia are already elderly civilizations, sinking into their twilights. The Trojan War has been fought, shattering the greatness of Asia Minor and enhancing the power of Mycenae. Mighty Crete, ripped by earthquakes and pirate raiders, is slipping into decline. The powerful nations of the Near East and the eastern Mediterranean islands are moving toward their final days, while new leaders are about to emerge and reshape the patterns of power. The glory of Greece and the grandeur of Rome are just on the horizon, and with them Europe will move from prehistory to history.

Greece and Rome, though, are Mediterranean in

220 outlook. Mountain walls cut them off from the rest of Europe. North of the Alps, a thousand years of prehistory still remains. While first the Greeks and then the Romans are snatching power from the dying civilizations to the east, ruder empires are emerging north of the Alps.

For the first time, we can call a prehistoric European people by its own rightful name. The names we have used up to this point are those invented by archaeologists. We do not know what names the Aurignacians and Gravettians had for themselves, nor what were the true identities of the Beaker Folk and Battle-Axe People. But we know that the last prehistoric masters of central and western Europe called themselves the Celts.

We know because Greek historians tell us so. By 450 B.C., prehistory and history bordered one another so closely in Europe that a Greek named Herodotus could write an account of the barbarians who lived to the west and north, beyond the Alps. He gave them the name of *Keltoi,* or Celts, which he said was how they referred to themselves. They were tall, fair-skinned blond people with blue eyes, quite different from the dark, short population of the Mediterranean world. To Herodotus, they were little more than savages, but in his eyes any man who could not speak the noble Greek tongue was not really civilized. Actually, the Celts had developed a complex and elaborate civilization, which we call prehistoric only because it lacked a written language.

The Celts were aggressive, forever in search of new territory. A few years after the death of Herodotus they began coming through the Alpine passes into Italy. The Romans, who in 400 B.C. had not yet begun to build their world empire, called them *Galli,* or Gauls. Roman historians recognized the existence of a confederation of Gauls stretching across Europe from the Alps to the Atlantic. When the Gauls stormed Rome in 381 B.C., the city burned helplessly and the defeated Romans were forced to pay a ransom for their freedom. An arrogant Gaul threw his sword on the scale as the ransom was being weighed out, crying, *"Vae victis!"*—"Woe to the vanquished." It was a phrase the Romans remembered well, and made the Gauls themselves hear in misery.

As Rome grew, the Celtic Gauls had to give ground, first south of the Alps, then in virtually all of Europe. By the time of the Caesars, the Celts were simply one more conquered people under the heel of Rome. Only in Britain and Ireland, which they had occupied as Roman power forced them from Germany and France, did they still survive in numbers, and eventually Celtic Britain was conquered too. By the time of Christ, history and prehistory had become one in Europe.

The Celts, then, figured in the writings of contemporary historians. They never needed to be rediscovered as, say, the Beaker Folk had been. The task of the archaeologists was simply to match the record of buried artifacts with the accounts of Herodotus and the Roman chroniclers.

A great Celtic site was discovered in 1846—by accident, as such things often happen. At the Austrian town of Hallstatt, on the northern flank of the Alps, a road was being built, and a workman turned up a human skull with a bronze earring. Some quick digging produced a complete skeleton, and then another, a beautiful bronze bracelet, and a pottery vase. It was an ancient cemetery. Skeletons lay in neat rows, their arms by their sides, and nearly every one was decked with ornaments of bronze. Johann Georg Ramsauer, the manager of a local salt mine, took charge of the job of uncovering the Hallstatt cemetery. Financed by a grant from a museum in Vienna, he worked for nineteen years and ultimately opened nearly a thousand graves. More than half of these were contained skeletons, but in 468 of them the bodies had been completely or partly cremated.

From these graves came thousands of objects, many of bronze but some of iron. Amber necklaces were plentiful, and there were earrings of gold and some vessels of glass. The most common articles were brooches, pins, and belt buckles. Hundreds of daggers and short swords were found. It seemed that the Iron Age people of Hallstatt preferred to be buried with most of their earthly possessions.

We know today that the Hallstatt cemetery was in use between 1000 and 500 B.C., at a time when that part of Austria was occupied by the Celts. Then as now, Hallstatt was surrounded by valuable salt mines, on which its prosperity was based. Wherever salt was mined, trade routes met. In exchange for the salt of Hallstatt, merchants brought amber from Denmark, beads from Egypt, coral trinkets from the shores of the Red Sea, vases from Greece, furs from the northern lands. All these splendors found their way into the possession of the Celts of Hallstatt, and then into their graves.

The Celts had sprung from the older cultures of Europe some time after the mingling of Beaker Folk and Battle-Axe People and Neolithic farmers. They were farmers and herdsmen themselves, settled village dwellers who lived in sturdy rectangular wooden houses. Though at first they made their tools and weapons from bronze, they quickly learned of the new metal, iron.

The first ironworkers lived in Asia Minor about 1400 B.C. They used the natural iron that fell from the skies in meteorites—hammering it into shape. Iron was much harder than bronze and took a finer edge; but it was a long time before men knew how to build fires hot enough to melt iron so that it could be cast. They were limited to what they could fashion by hammering the metal. A warlike nation known as the Hittites, armed with iron swords, struck terror into Egypt around 1300 B.C. and made other nations eager to get such weapons for themselves. In another few centuries, the use of iron spread into Europe, and by 900 B.C. even the Celts of Hallstatt were in the Iron Age.

The Hallstatt cemetery has given its name to an entire epoch of Celtic life. During the Hallstatt period, certain chieftains amassed great wealth and were buried with impressive pomp. The contents of their funeral mounds show the luxuriousness of Hallstatt life. Whole chariots were sometimes buried with them—light, handsome, four-wheeled vehicles with iron-covered hubs and wheelspokes. In 1953, a grave of this sort was found in a late Hallstatt-period cemetery in France. The tomb, ten feet square, lay under a mound of great size. Surely it was the resting place of a Celtic princess or queen. The body of a woman about thirty years old lay in a chariot with iron-shod wheels. Around her skull was a gold diadem weighing more than a pound, lovingly crafted. Brooches of iron and bronze, anklets and armlets, bronze bowls, two Greek cups, and an enormous bronze wine vessel a yard across and five feet high, also were in the tomb—everything made with master workmanship.

A much humbler device also stems from Hallstatt times: the safety pin, or *fibula*, as prehistorians call it. The Celts seem to have invented this useful item, fashioning safety pins first from bronze and later from iron. Though highly ornate and of large size, the Hallstatt *fibulae* worked exactly as modern safety pins do. (*Photograph, page 200.*)

224     A different phase of Celtic life began about 500 B.C. and is known to archaeologists as the La Tène period. Its type-site was discovered in 1857 by Friedrich Schwab, a wealthy Swiss hobbyist-archaeologist. Schwab was actually searching for pile dwellings, for this was the time when Ferdinand Keller was announcing his Lake Dweller discoveries. Working at the northeastern end of Lake Neuchâtel in Switzerland, Schwab came upon a submerged mound at the place where a river fed into the lake. This mound was locally known as La Tène, "The Shallow Place." It proved to contain a hoard of lances, swords, and spearheads, some still in their scabbards. When the rust was cleaned from them, they proved to be of iron, and thus much later than the era of the Lake Dwellers. They were slim, graceful weapons whose hilts were often attractively decorated with twining ornamentation. Further research showed that the La Tène culture was widespread in western Europe and represented a refinement of the Hallstatt Celtic culture, marked by new trends in craftsmanship.

La Tène sites abound with elegant iron swords and daggers and with safety pins of ever more ingenious pattern. The first scissors known to archaeologists were made by these people. They consisted simply of a bar of iron with a blade at each end, bent double so that by clasping the hand one could force one blade to slide past the other. Another La Tène novelty was the lock and key.

The Celts of the Greek and Roman historians have by now been clearly associated with the artifacts of the Hallstatt and La Tène epochs. Theirs was a rich and interesting culture, which lies right at the artificial border between prehistory and history. We do not need to reconstruct their way of life from tools and weapons and scraps of bone alone, for we have Herodotus to tell us what they were like. And so the

Celts stand at the end of the story of prehistoric Europe. Even their faces are familiar to us. No museum gallery of Roman sculpture is complete without a marble image of a warrior of Gaul—the Celtic foe, fierce and brawny and yet always a noble figure, a barbarian but not a savage. When we can look upon the face of prehistoric man, we are passing beyond the realm of archaeology.

We need not even rely on marble portraits. If we journey to Denmark today, we can see prehistoric man in the flesh, every fold and wrinkle of skin preserved, for actual men of the Iron Age lie in Danish museums, like wanderers out of time.

They are the bodies from the bogs. The bogs of northwest Europe contain humic acid, which has a preserving effect on organic matter. A corpse thrust into such a bog will retain its lifelike appearance indefinitely. About a hundred such bodies have been found in the Danish bogs and those of Holland and northwest Germany. One of them dates from recent times—about A.D. 1700—and several come from the Middle Ages. The rest have been dated to Celtic times, twenty or twenty-five centuries ago. Though not Celtic-speaking people themselves, the northern Europeans of that time were strongly under the influence of the contemporary La Tène culture of France and central Europe.

Two brothers cutting peat at the Danish moor called Tollund found such a bog corpse in May 1950. It lay under seven feet of peat at the bottom of the bog, about fifty yards from firm ground. The body was on its right side, the knees drawn up against the chest. The first thing the diggers did was notify the police in the nearby town of Silkeborg—for who could be sure that this was a prehistoric burial, and not the body of some recent murder victim?

The police sped to the scene, but quickly saw that

226 this was work for archaeologists, not for them. They telephoned the university in the much larger city of Aarhus, twenty-five miles away. Peter Glob, a leading Danish archaeologist, happened to be lecturing there that day. He set out at once for the bog of Tollund.

The road from Aarhus to Silkeborg is almost completely straight, and passes through flat farm country. No speed limits are imposed on automobile traffic. Professor Glob's account of the discovery does not tell us how quickly he got from Aarhus to Silkeborg, but quite probably he set a new record for the route. From there to Tollund was another six miles. When he had viewed the bog corpse, he knew it was a major discovery.

"A foot and a shoulder protruded," he wrote, "perfectly preserved but dark brown in color like the surrounding peat, which had dyed the skin. Carefully we removed more peat, and a bowed head came into view. As dusk fell, we saw in the fading light a man take shape before us. He was curled up, with legs drawn under him and arms bent, resting on his side as if asleep. His eyes were peacefully shut; his brows were furrowed and his mouth showed a slightly irritated quirk as if he were not overpleased by this unexpected disturbance of his rest." The entire block of peat in which he lay embedded was cut free and placed in a crate for shipment to the National Museum in Copenhagen.

Examination there revealed that the head, the feet, and the underside of the corpse were perfectly preserved. The arms and hands had been partly destroyed by the diggers, and the upper side of the body showed signs of decay. The body was naked except for a belt of hide and a small peaked cap, made of eight pieces of leather sewed together. Around the neck was a braided leather noose. Tollund Man had been hanged.

A full autopsy was performed. The internal organs were found to be intact, and Tollund Man's last meal remained in his stomach, only partly digested. He had last eaten twelve to twenty-four hours before his death, and his meal had consisted of porridge made from barley, flax seed, and grass seed. He had eaten no meat. Apparently he had died in winter, when no fresh plant food was available.

Why had he been slain?

Perhaps he had committed some terrible crime. But Tollund Man did not have the face of a criminal, if there is such a thing. His sensitive, intelligent features might have been those of a poet or a priest. And the striking calmness of his expression was not the look one would expect to find on the face of a criminal being hanged.

Archaeologists think that Tollund Man was the willing victim of an Iron Age ritual of death. They suspect that he was given by his village as a sacrifice to the gods, in a wintertime rite to insure the coming of spring's fertility. Chosen for this grim honor, he may have spent his final months in ease and comfort, spared from daily labor. Then, as the festival time approached, he abstained from eating meat, dining only on the grain porridge that may have had some mystic significance in the worship of the harvest deity. On the last day, with the midwinter rite coming to its somber climax, he submitted peacefully as the noose was knotted round his neck. After the execution, his body was carried to the bog, where it slumbered for twenty centuries until the spades of diggers disturbed its rest.

All this is speculation. But it rests on our knowledge of ancient harvest rituals, and on the evidence of Tollund Man himself.

Two years later, in the spring of 1952, Peter Glob once again set out from Aarhus to inspect a bog

228  corpse. This one was found near the village of Grauballe, not far from Tollund. Workmen cutting peat uncovered the neck, shoulder, and head of a man. Under Dr. Glob's supervision, the body was taken to the Prehistoric Museum in Aarhus, where the peat covering was carefully removed.

Grauballe Man was lying in the bog with his left leg and left arm outstretched, his right leg and arm sharply bent. Other bog corpses had previously been found in the same position, suggesting a ritualistic form of burial. The Grauballe body was completely naked. His head had been crushed, and his throat was slit from ear to ear. As a result, he did not have the unearthly tranquility of Tollund Man; his mouth was agape and his features contorted.

It had not been possible to preserve the entire Tollund corpse. Like any waterlogged object, it would have cracked and crumbled if allowed to dry out, and so could be kept only through an involved and expensive process. This would have required repeated baths in pure alcohol, until the water in the flesh was completely replaced by alcohol, and then a coating of paraffin wax added as a final preservative. Because of the problems posed by this technique, all that could be saved of Tollund Man was the head and neck, with its marvelously expressive face and the sinister marks of the noose. (*Photograph, page 200.*)

However, Tollund Man had been only partially complete when found. Grauballe Man was virtually intact, down to his fingerprints and the three-day stubble of beard on his chin. The technicians of the Aarhus Museum were determined to save the body in its entirety. They devised a process for soaking it in a vat of water and oak bark, which contains tannic acid. For eighteen months the tanning process continued, until the skin was turned to fine leather.

Then the body was dried and coated with linseed oil, **229** and placed on exhibition.

Grauballe Man occupies a room of his own in the Aarhus Museum, lying on his side, as he was found, within a glass case. He is not a pretty sight, this twisted, mutilated victim of Iron Age execution. Yet it is hard to leave the darkened room in which he lies. Here is no cold display of stone blades, no case of skulls and ribs, no rusty iron axes—none of the usual museum offerings of prehistoric times. Here lies nothing but a man, who was born before Christ and whose battered form is a vivid reminder that those cultures we call prehistoric were the work of human beings of our own kind.

It is an even more moving experience to go upstairs in the small, cluttered museum at Silkeborg, to the little case where Tollund Man is kept. Since only the head and neck remain, at first glance the impact is slight. Then, leaning over, we peer closely, staring at the solemn, thoughtful face of Tollund Man, his high forehead furrowed with a frown, his lips compressed, his eyes forever closed. We look at that face, the face of prehistoric man, and we see ourselves.

# FOR FURTHER READING

In the following list, books marked with a single asterisk will be particularly useful to young readers because of their text or illustrations. Books marked with a double asterisk are technical works and early sources not likely to be of much interest to the general reader.

GENERAL PREHISTORIC BACKGROUND

Edward Bacon: *Digging for History.* John Day, New York, 1961.

*Geoffrey Bibby: *Four Thousand Years Ago.* Knopf, New York, 1962.

*——— *The Testimony of the Spade.* Knopf, New York, 1956.

**Marcellin Boule and Henri V. Vallois: *Fossil Men.* Translated by Michael Bullock. Dryden Press, New York, 1957.

Richard Carrington: *A Million Years of Man.* World, Cleveland and New York, 1963. Mentor paperback edition, 1964.

V. Gordon Childe: *Man Makes Himself.* New American Library, New York, 1951.

——— *What Happened in History.* Pelican Books, Harmondsworth, England, 1942.

**Carleton S. Coon: *The Origin of Races.* Knopf, New York, 1962.

Glyn Daniel: *The Idea of Prehistory.* World, Cleveland and New York, 1963.

Jacquetta and Christopher Hawkes: *Prehistoric Britain.* Pelican Books, Harmondsworth, England, 1943.

**Jacquetta Hawkes and Sir Leonard Woolley: *Prehistory and the Beginnings of Civilization.* Harper & Row, New York and Evanston, 1963.

**Robert F. Heizer, editor: *Man's Discovery of His Past.* Prentice-Hall, New Jersey, 1962.

**Frank C. Hibben: *Prehistoric Man in Europe*. University of Oklahoma Press, Norman, 1958.

**Alfred L. Kroeber: *Anthropology* (revised edition). Harcourt, Brace & World, New York, 1948.

**———, editor: *Anthropology Today*. University of Chicago Press, Chicago, 1953.

George Grant McCurdy: *The Coming of Man*. The University Society, Inc., New York, 1932.

**L. S. Palmer: *Man's Journey Through Time*. Hutchinson, London, 1957.

*Stuart Piggott, editor: *The Dawn of Civilization*. McGraw-Hill, New York, 1961.

*Robert Silverberg: *Man Before Adam*. Macrae Smith, Philadelphia, 1964.

Herbert Wendt: *In Search of Adam*. Houghton Mifflin, Boston, 1956.

S. E. Winbolt: *Britain B.C.* Pelican Books, Harmondsworth, England, 1943.


### THE UPPER PALEOLITHIC

*Georges Bataille: *Lascaux, or the Birth of Art*. Skira, New York, 1955.

*Alan Houghton Brodrick: *Father of Prehistory—The Abbé Henri Breuil*. William Morrow, New York, 1963.

**S. Giedion: *The Beginnings of Art*. Pantheon Books, New York, 1962.

H. L. Movius, Jr.: "Archaeology and the Earliest Art." *Scientific American*, Vol. 189, No. 2 (August 1953).

Philip E. L. Smith: "The Solutrean Culture." *Scientific American*, Vol. 211, No. 2 (August 1964).


### THE MESOLITHIC

Grahame Clark: "A Stone Age Hunters' Camp." *Scientific American*, Vol. 186, No. 5 (May 1952).

Johannes Iversen: "Forest Clearance in the Stone Age." *Scientific American*, Vol. 194, No. 3 (March 1956).

Marten Stenberger: *Sweden*. Thames and Hudson, London, 1963.

**Vladimir Dumitrescu: "Cascioarele: A Late Neolithic Settlement on the Lower Danube." *Archaeology*, Vol. 18, No. 1 (March 1965).

** Ferdinand Keller: *The Lake Dwellings of Switzerland*. Translated by John Edward Lee. Second edition. Longmans Green, London, 1878.

Hansjürgen Müller-Beck: "Prehistoric Swiss Lake Dwellers." *Scientific American*, Vol. 205, No. 6 (December 1961).

**Robert Munro: *The Lake Dwellings of Europe*. Cassell, London, 1890.

Robert J. Rodden: "An Early Neolithic Village in Greece." *Scientific American*, Vol. 212, No. 4 (April 1965).

MEGALITH BUILDERS AND THE BRONZE AGE

Emmanuel Anati: *Camonica Valley*. Translated by Linda Asher. Knopf, New York, 1961.

———— "Prehistoric Art in the Alps." *Scientific American*, Vol. 202, No. 1 (January 1960).

Holger Arbman: "Bronze Age Seen in Granite." *Natural History*, Vol. LXXIII, No. 9 (November 1964).

**O.G.S. Crawford: *The Eye Goddess*. Phoenix House, London, 1957.

Glyn Daniel: "Megaliths and Men." *Natural History*, Vol. LXXIII, No. 4 (April 1964).

———— *The Megalith Builders of Western Europe*. Hutchinson, London, 1958.

Gale Sieveking: "The Migration of the Megaliths." In *Vanished Civilizations*, edited by Edward Bacon. McGraw-Hill, New York, 1963.

STONEHENGE

R.J.C. Atkinson: *Stonehenge*. Hamish Hamilton, London, 1956.

———— *Stonehenge and Avebury.* Her Majesty's Stationery Office, London, 1959.

Jacquetta Hawkes: "Stonehenge." *Scientific American,* Vol. 188, No. 6 (June 1953).

Frank Stevens: "Stonehenge: Today and Yesterday." In *Smithsonian Institution Annual Report, 1940.* Government Printing Office, Washington, D.C., 1941.

THE IRON AGE

P. V. Glob: *Jernaldermanden fra Grauballe.* With English summary. Jysk Arkaeologisk Selskab, Aarhus, 1959.

T. G. E. Powell: *The Celts.* Thames and Hudson, London, 1958.

Knud Thorvildsen: *The Tollund Man.* Translated by Fred Mallet. Silkeborg Museum, Silkeborg, 1965.

# LIST OF ILLUSTRATIONS

Permission to reproduce the illustrations in this book has kindly been granted by the following:

The American Museum of Natural History, pages i, iv, vi, vii, viii (top), 45, 48, 50 and 51, 64 and 65, 68 and 69, 70 and 71, 84 and 85, 98 and 99, 140 and 141, 200 (top)
The French Government Tourist Office, pages ii, 193
Musée de l'Homme, Paris, page v
British Museum, London, page viii
Emmanuel Anati, *La Civilisation du Val Camonica*, page 184
Ministry of Public Building and Works, London, pages 194, 197, 205
Ministry of Public Building and Works, Edinburgh, page 195
Ashmolean Museum, Cambridge, England, page 196 (top)
Danish National Museum, page 196 (bottom)
Barbara Silverberg, pages 198, 199
Silkeborg Museum, Denmark, page 200 (bottom)

# INDEX